Gal Gadot Coloring Book

Powerful Female Icon and Wonder Woman Star, Beautiful Sex Symbol and Hot Model, Feminism Inspired Adult Coloring Book

June Hopkins

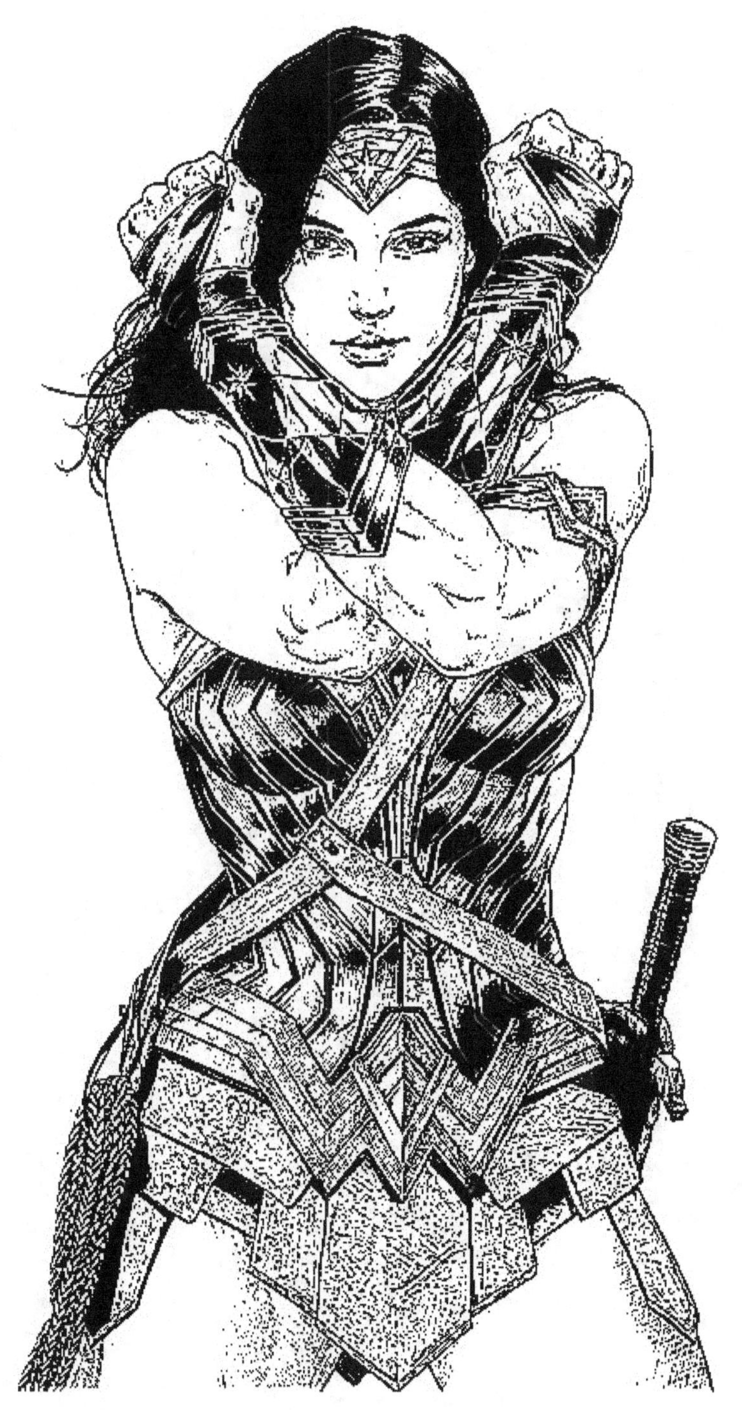

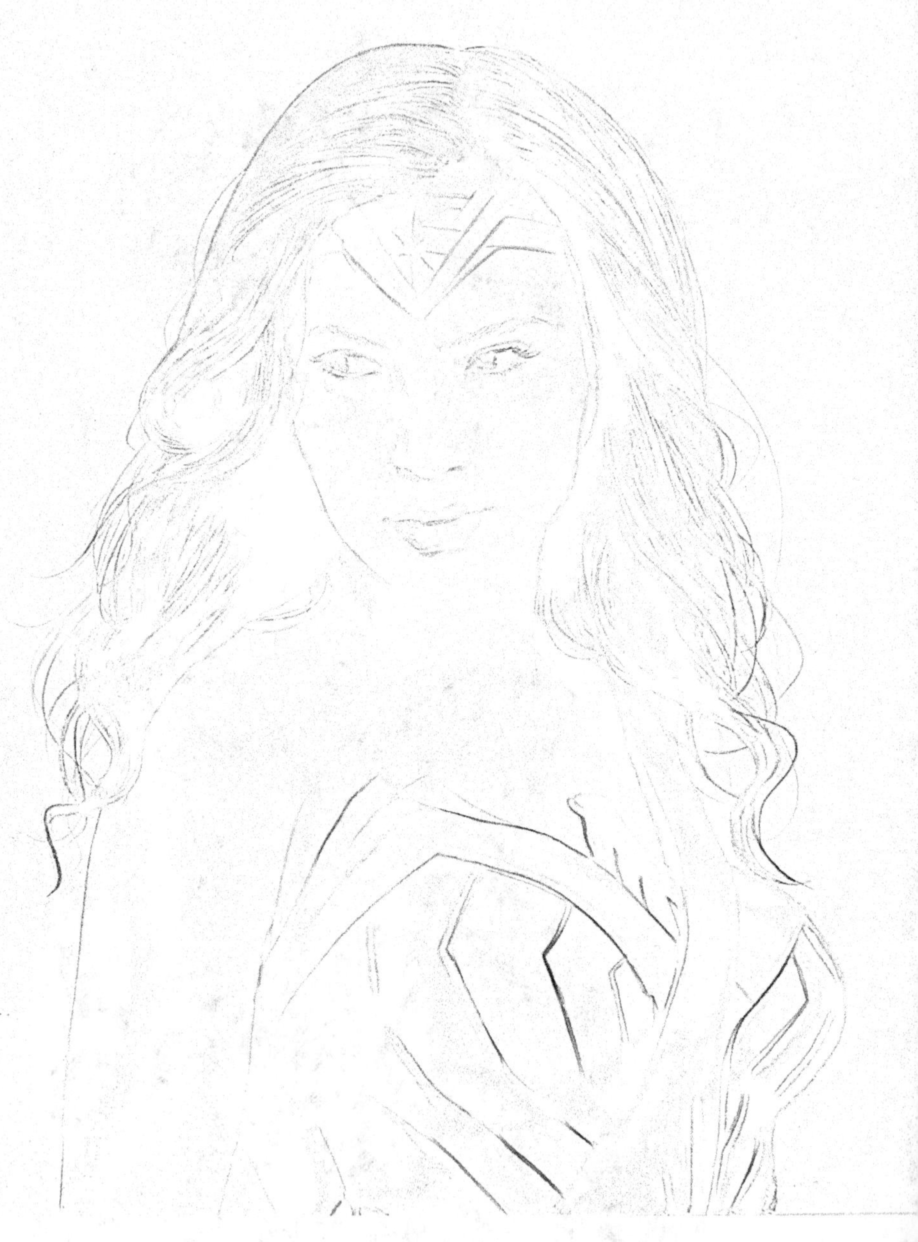

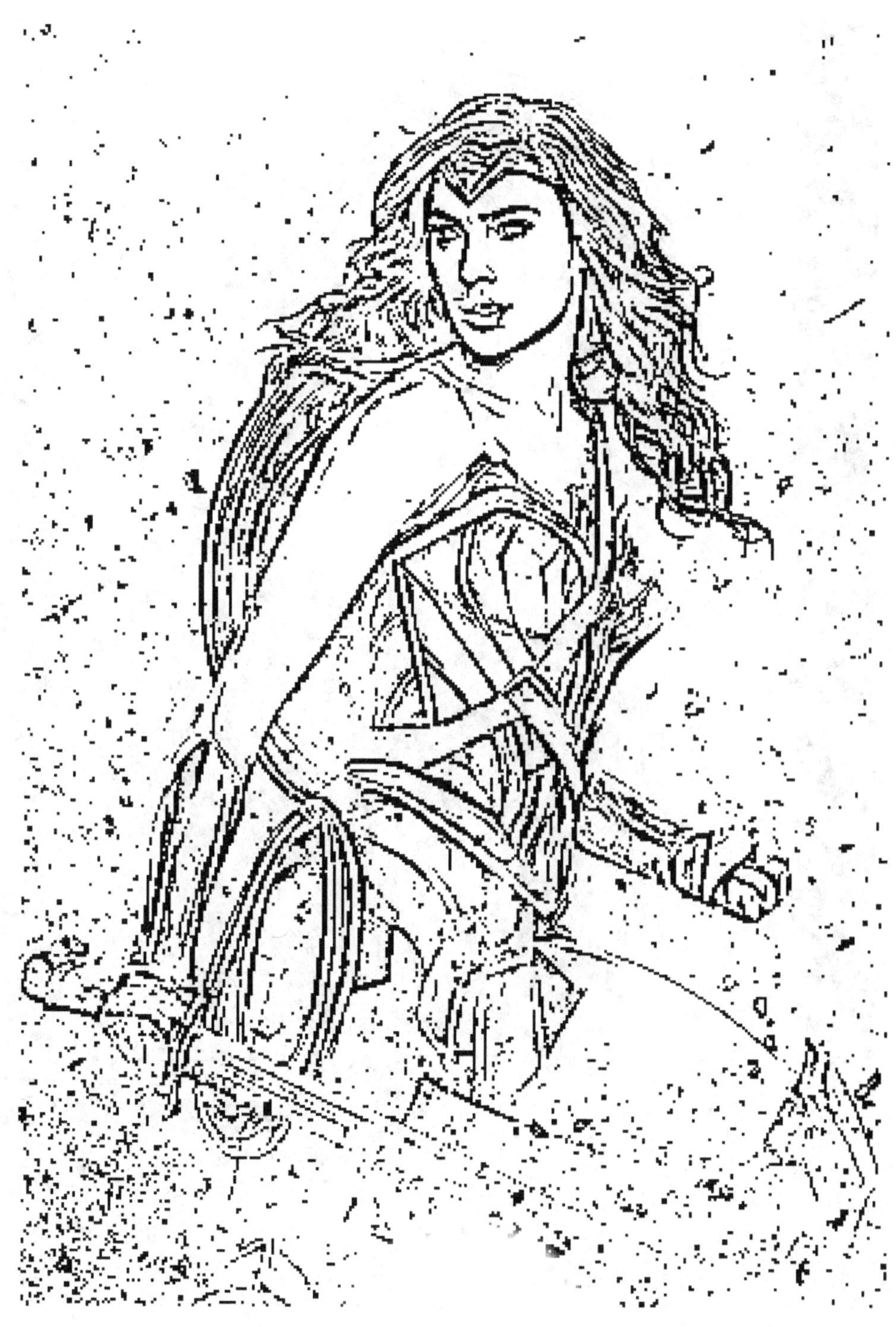

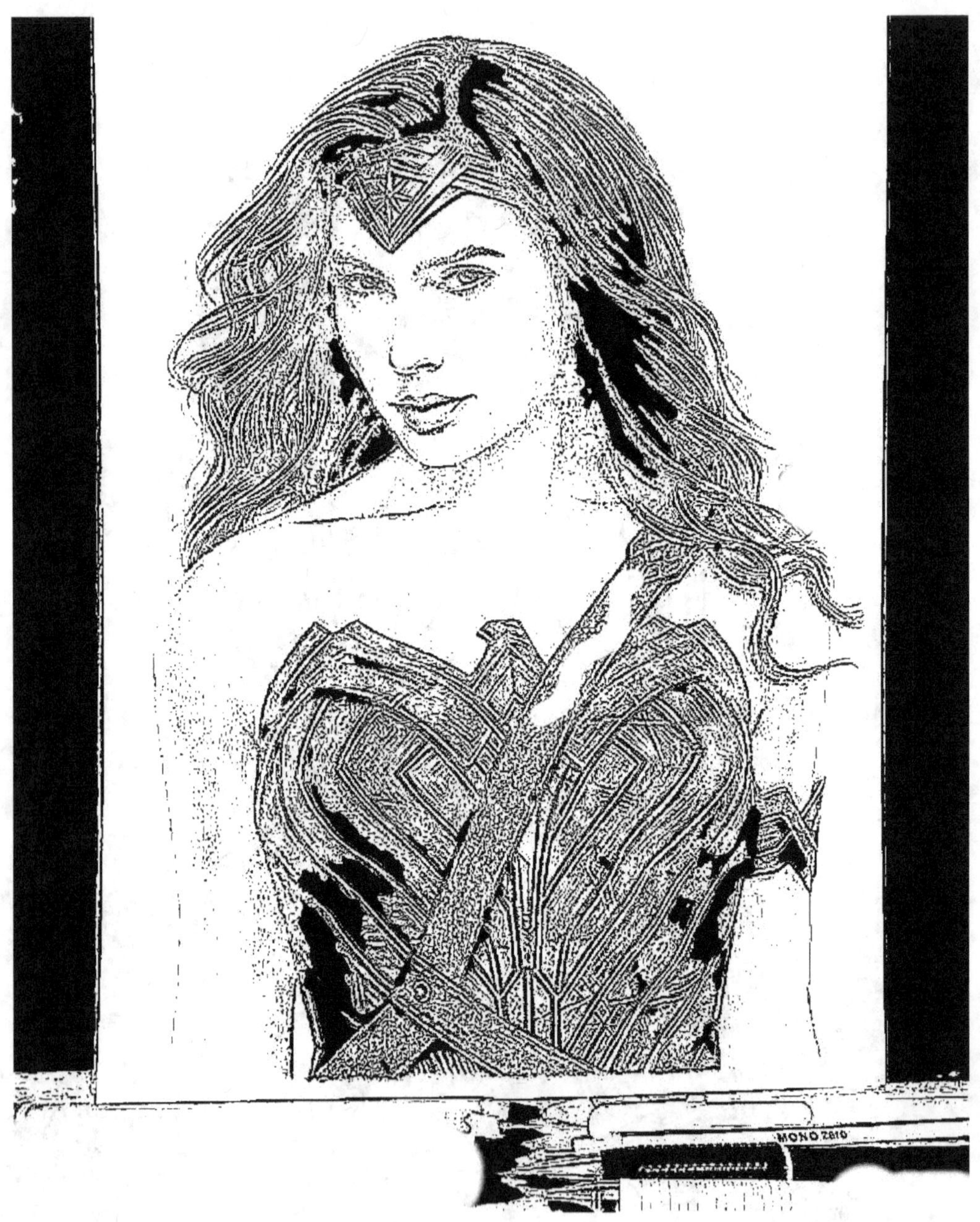

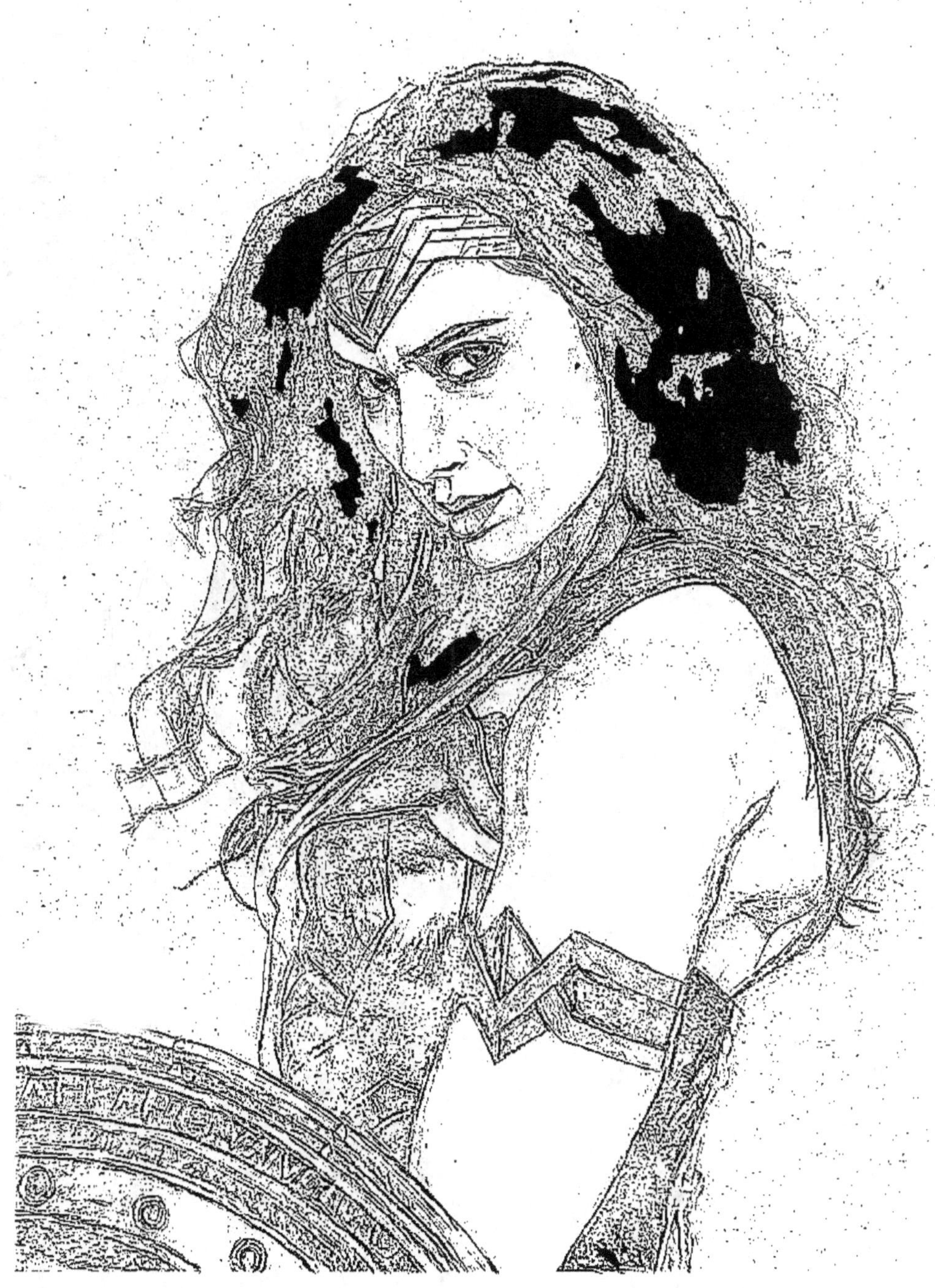

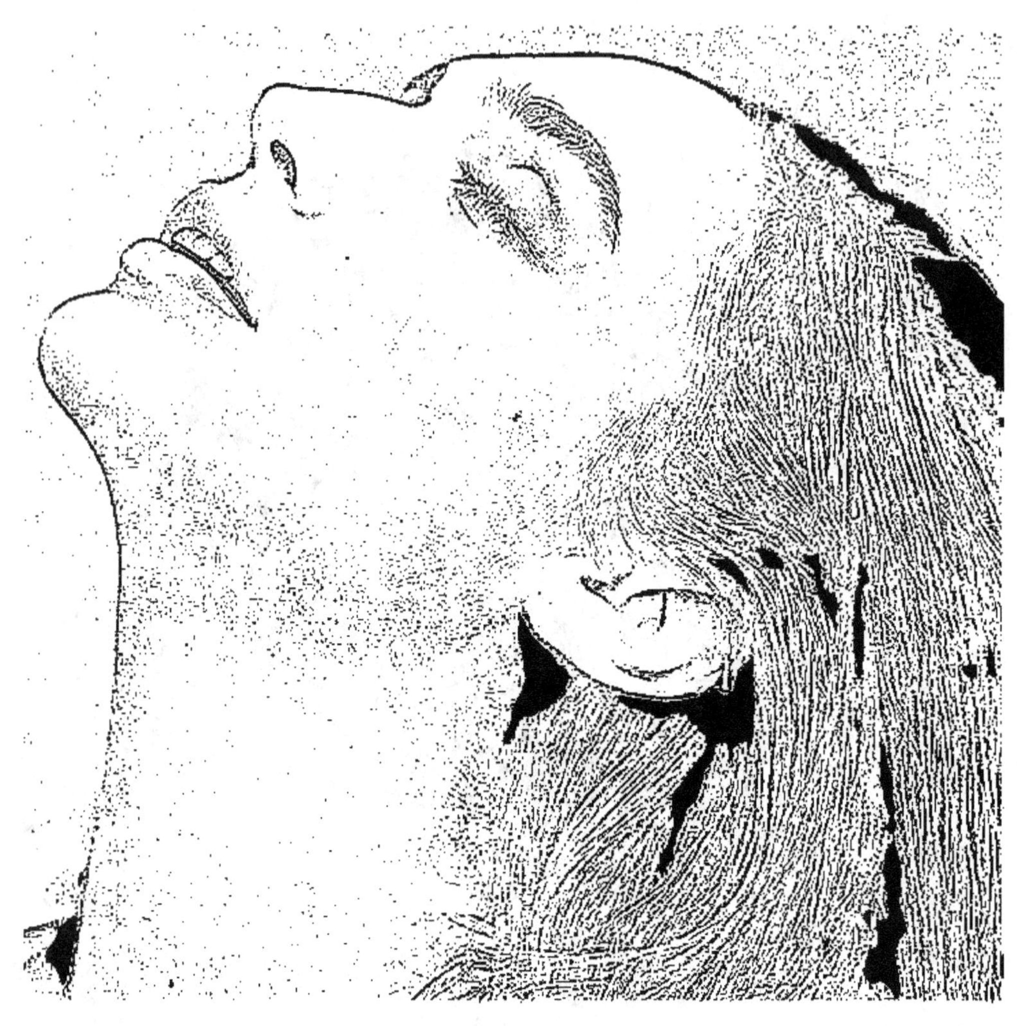

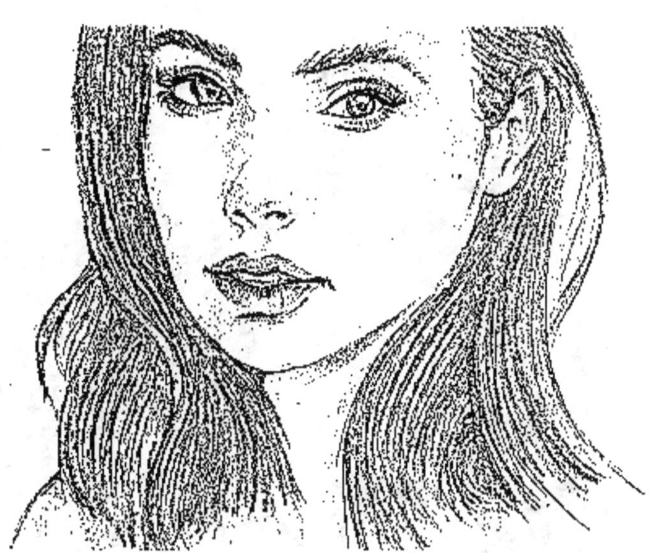

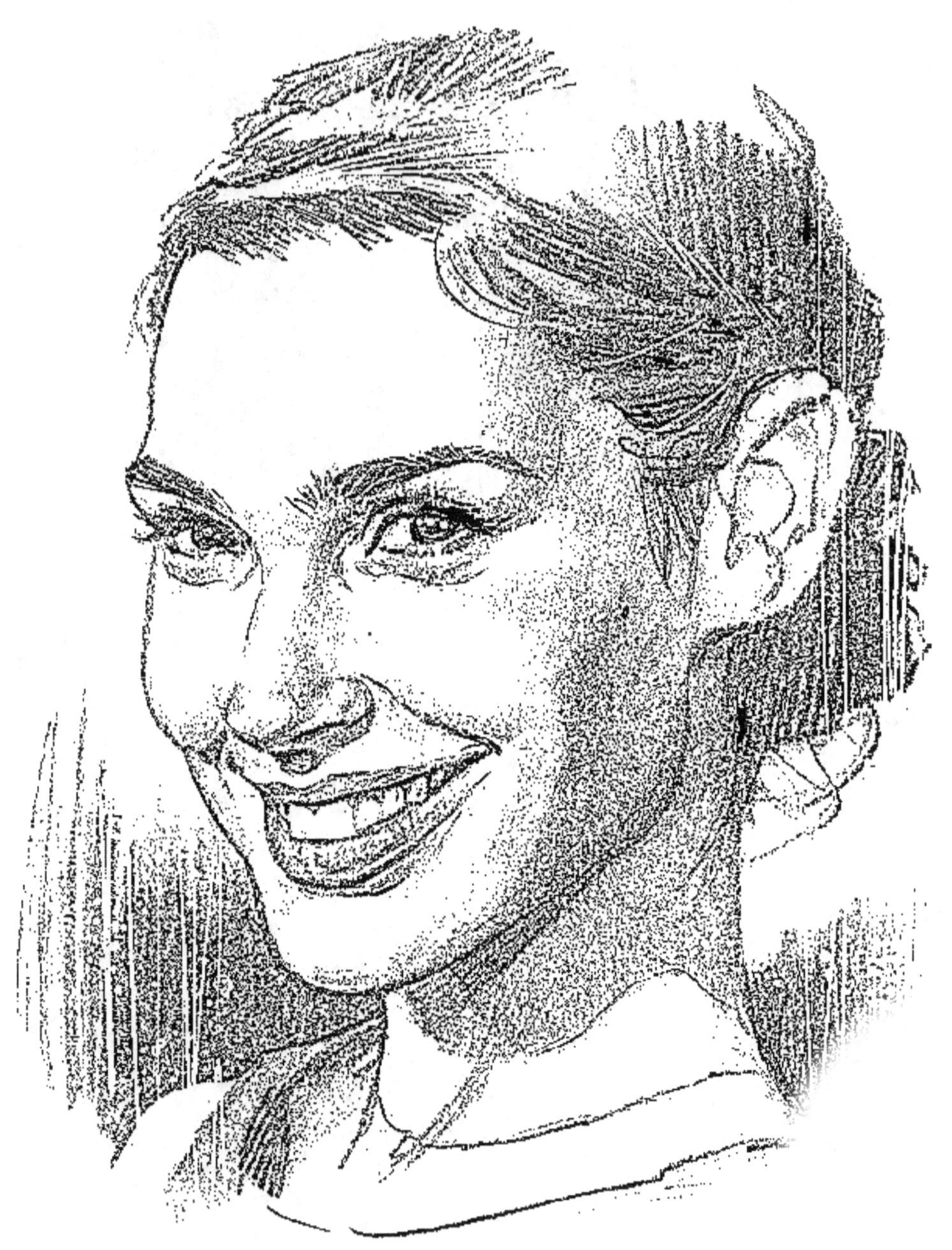

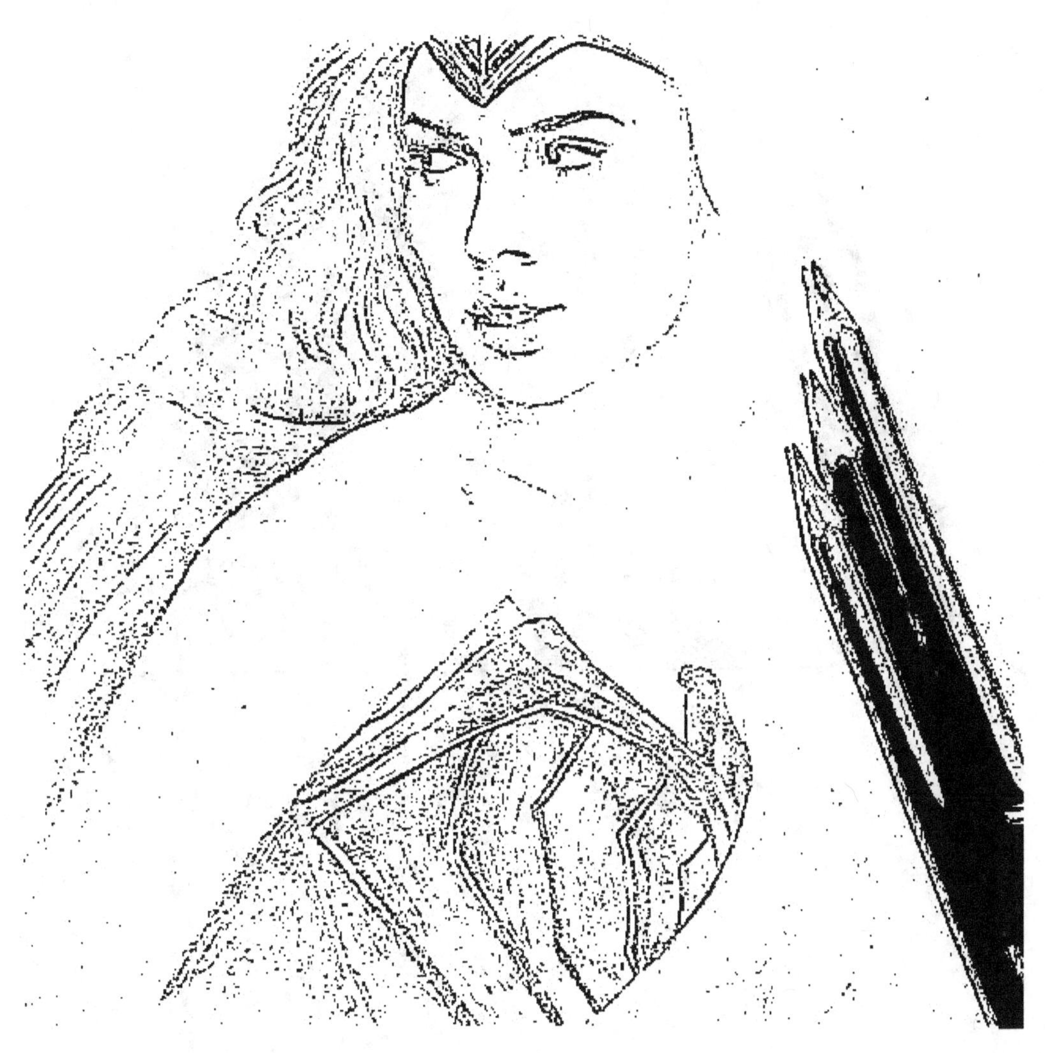

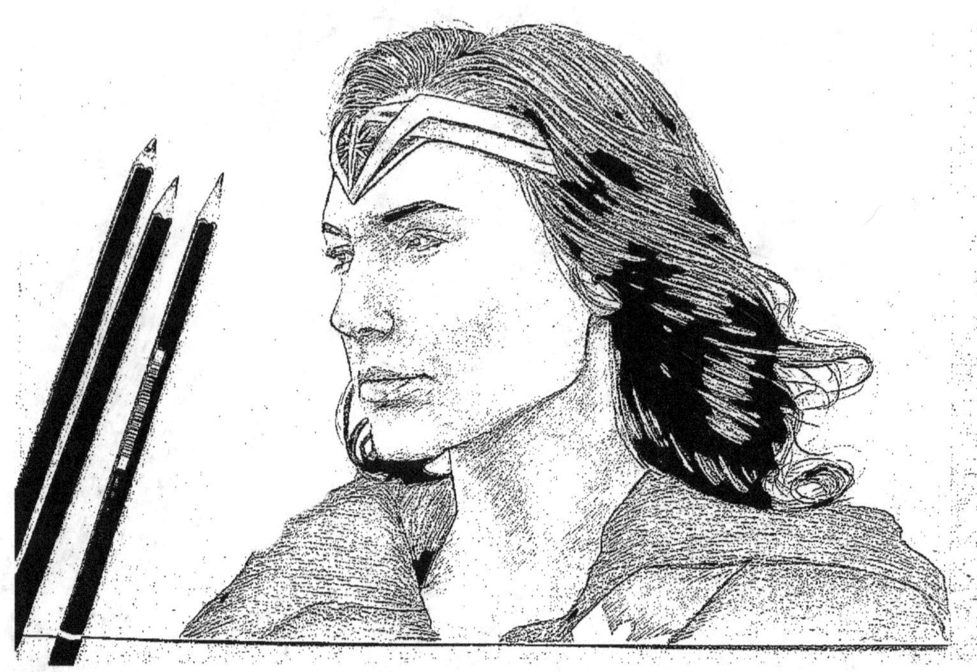

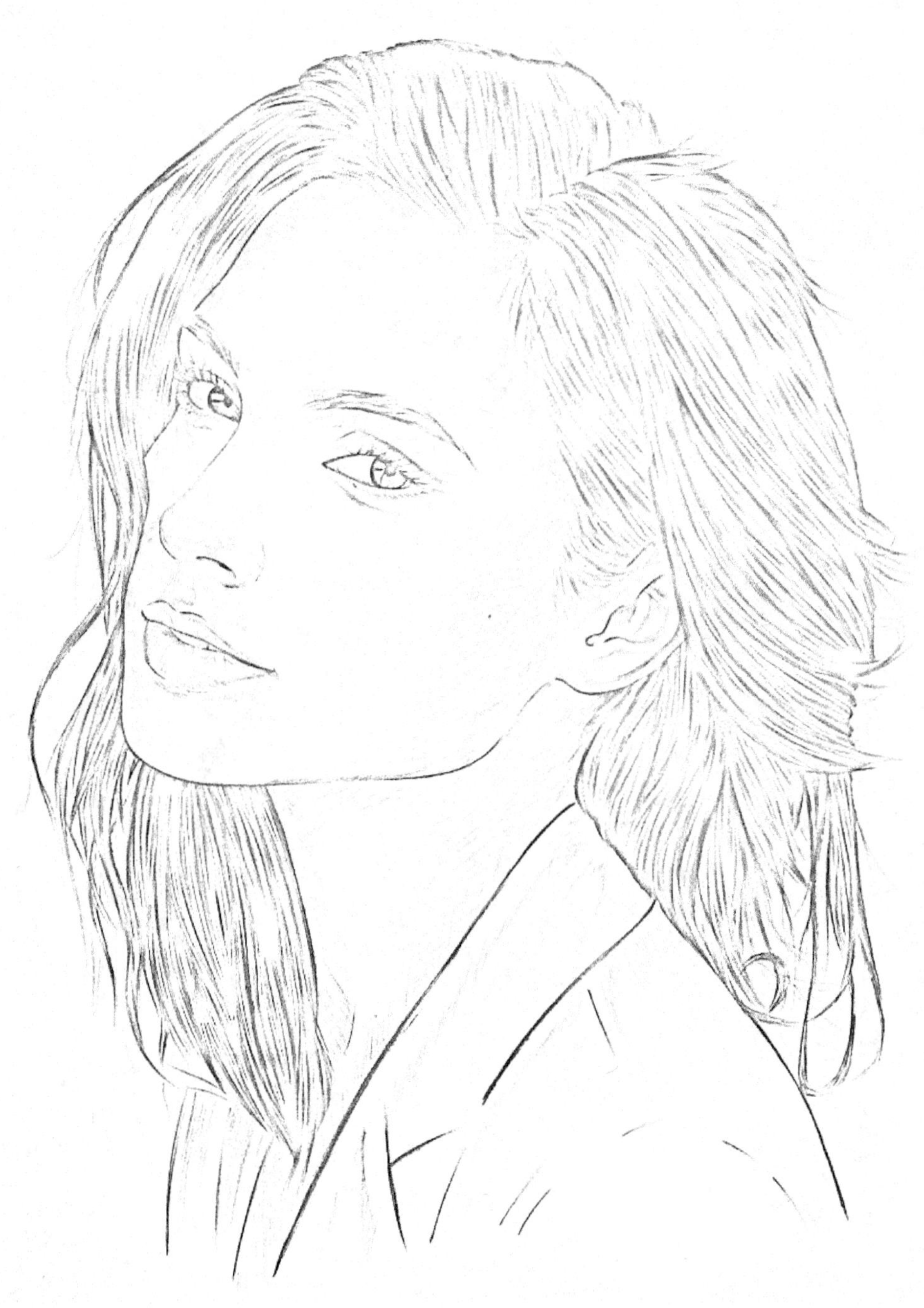

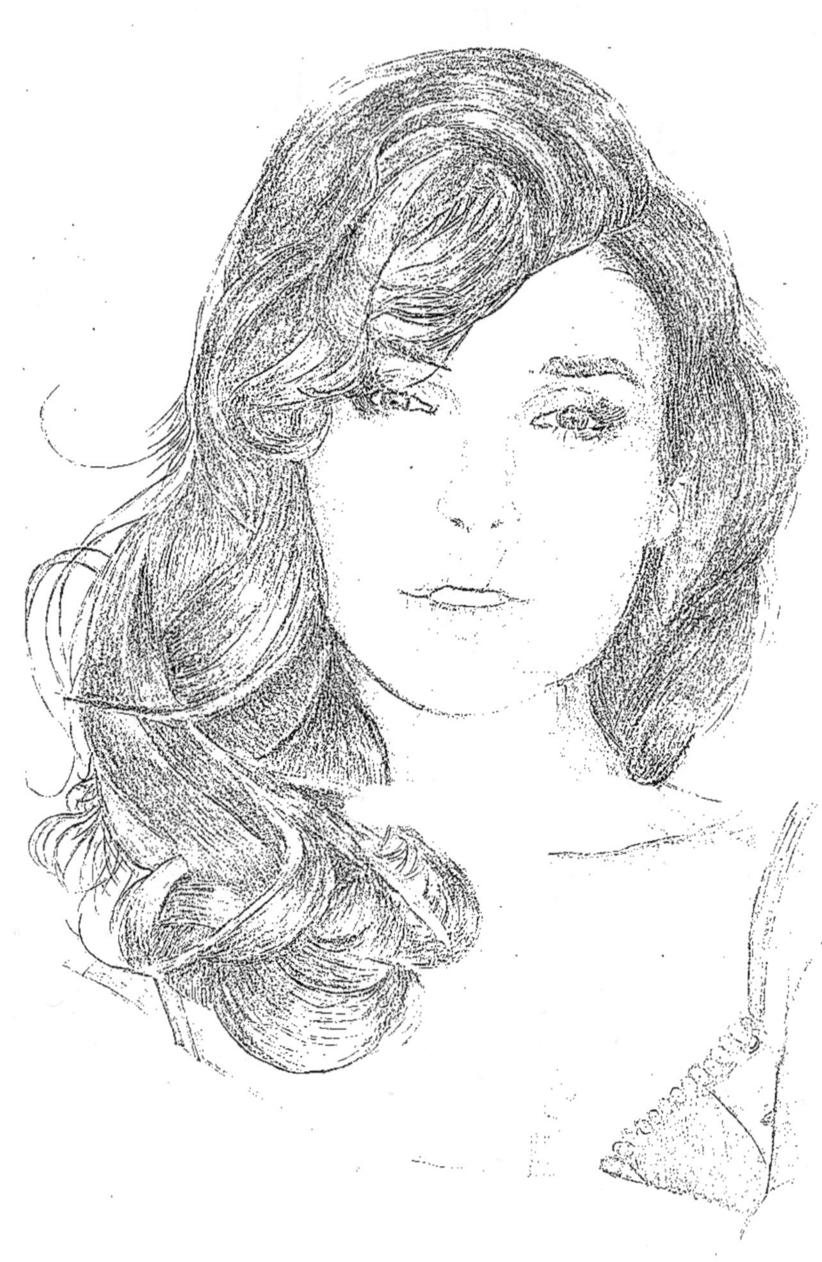

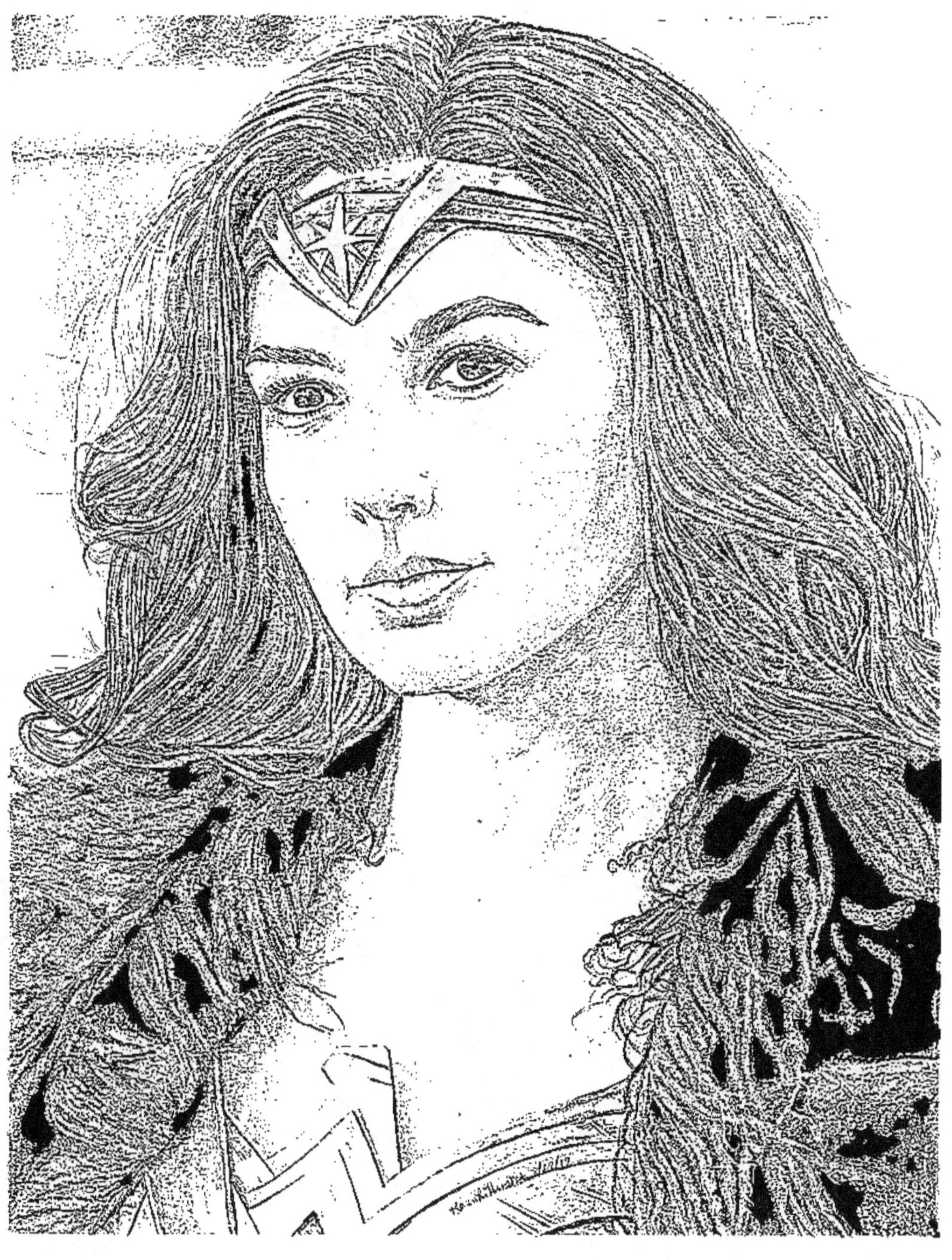

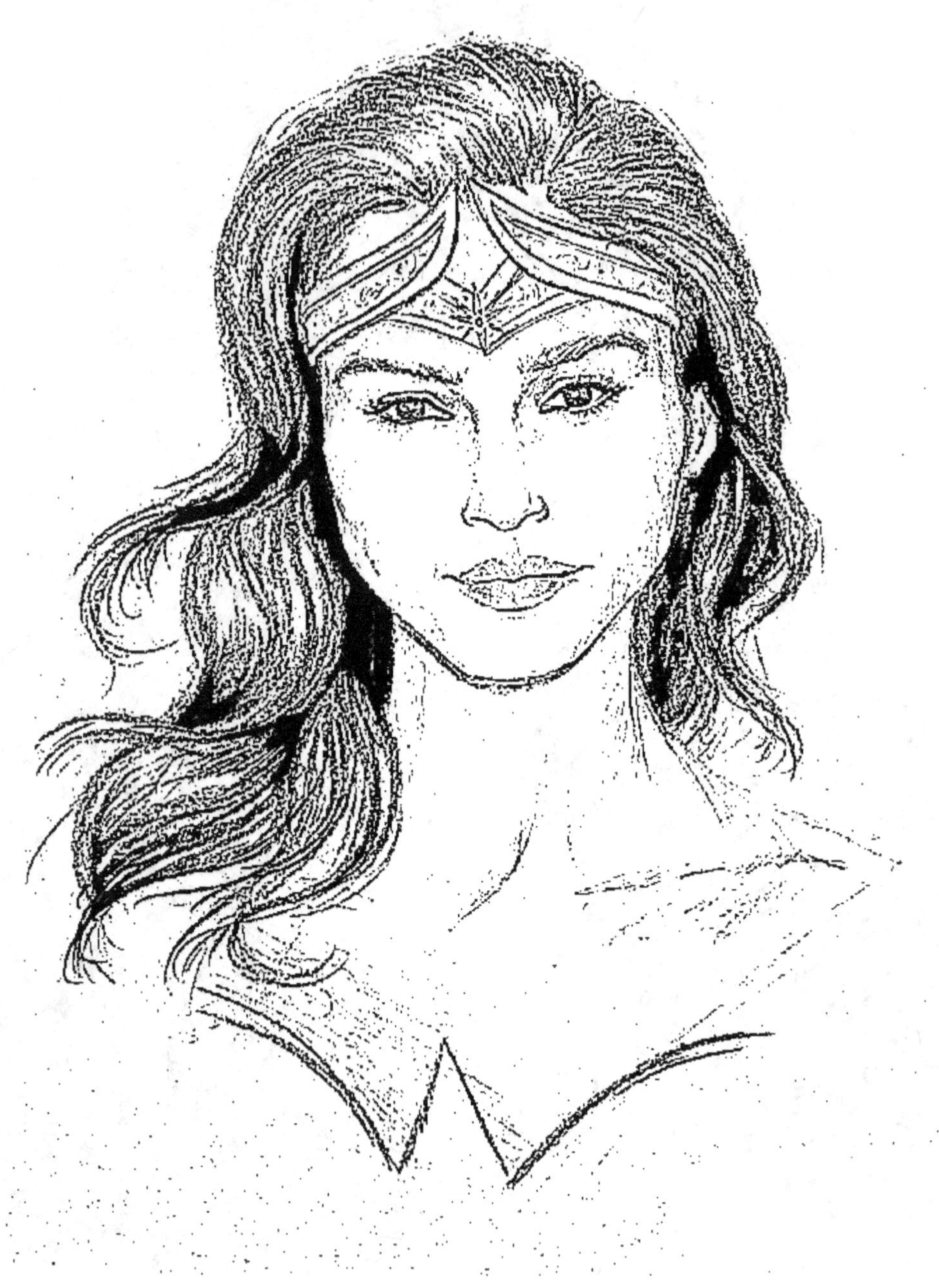

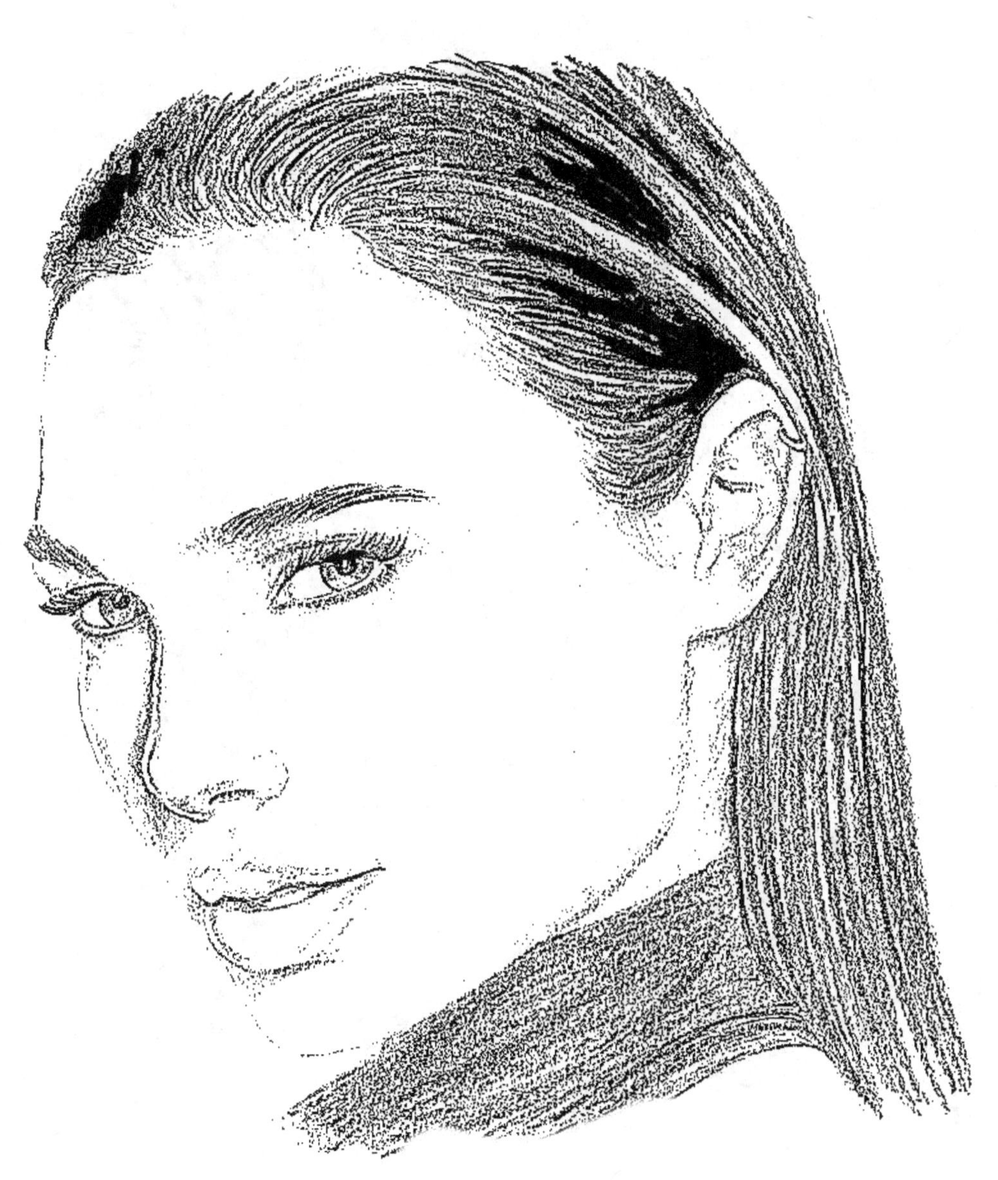

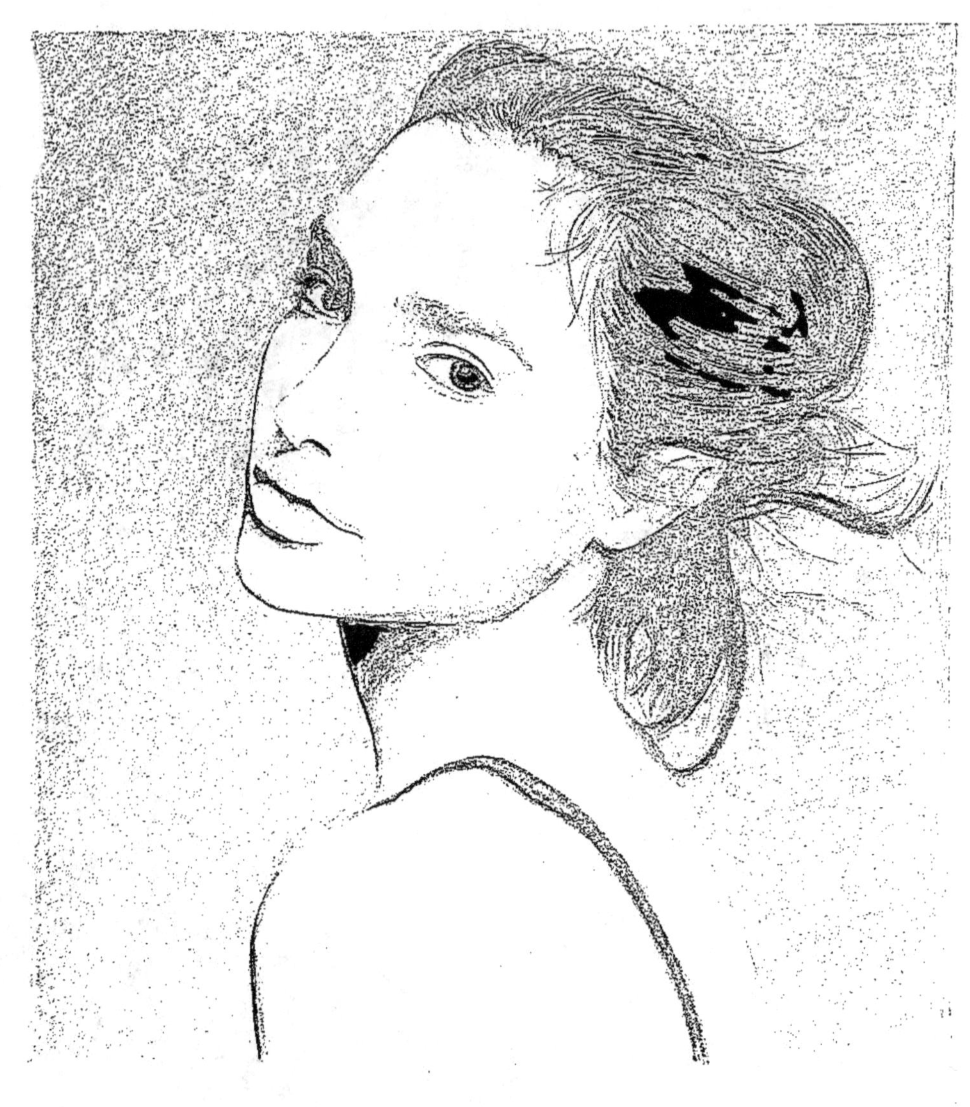

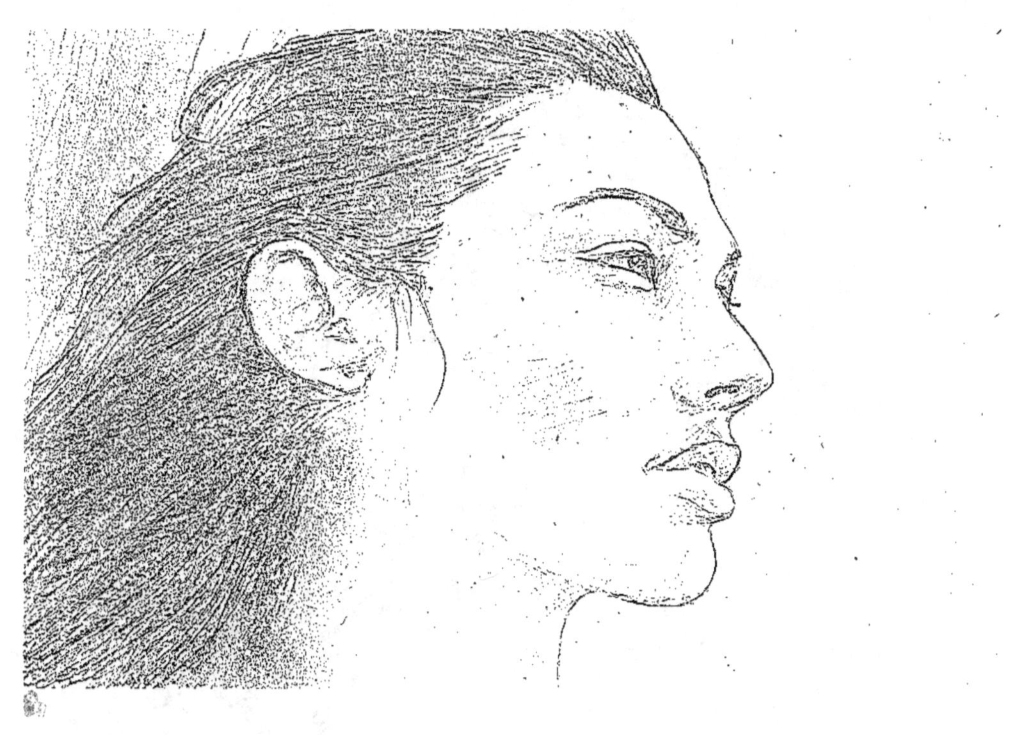

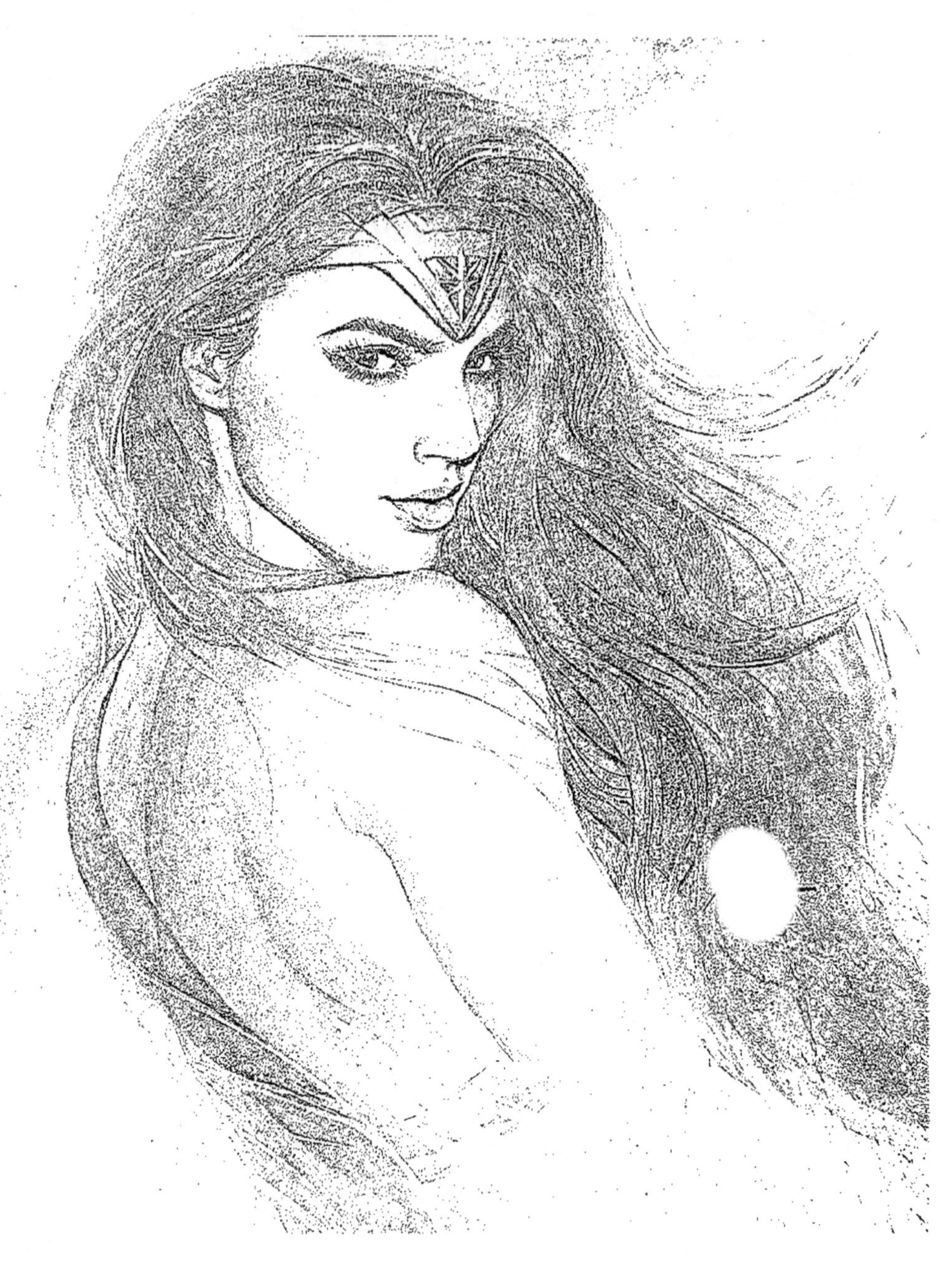

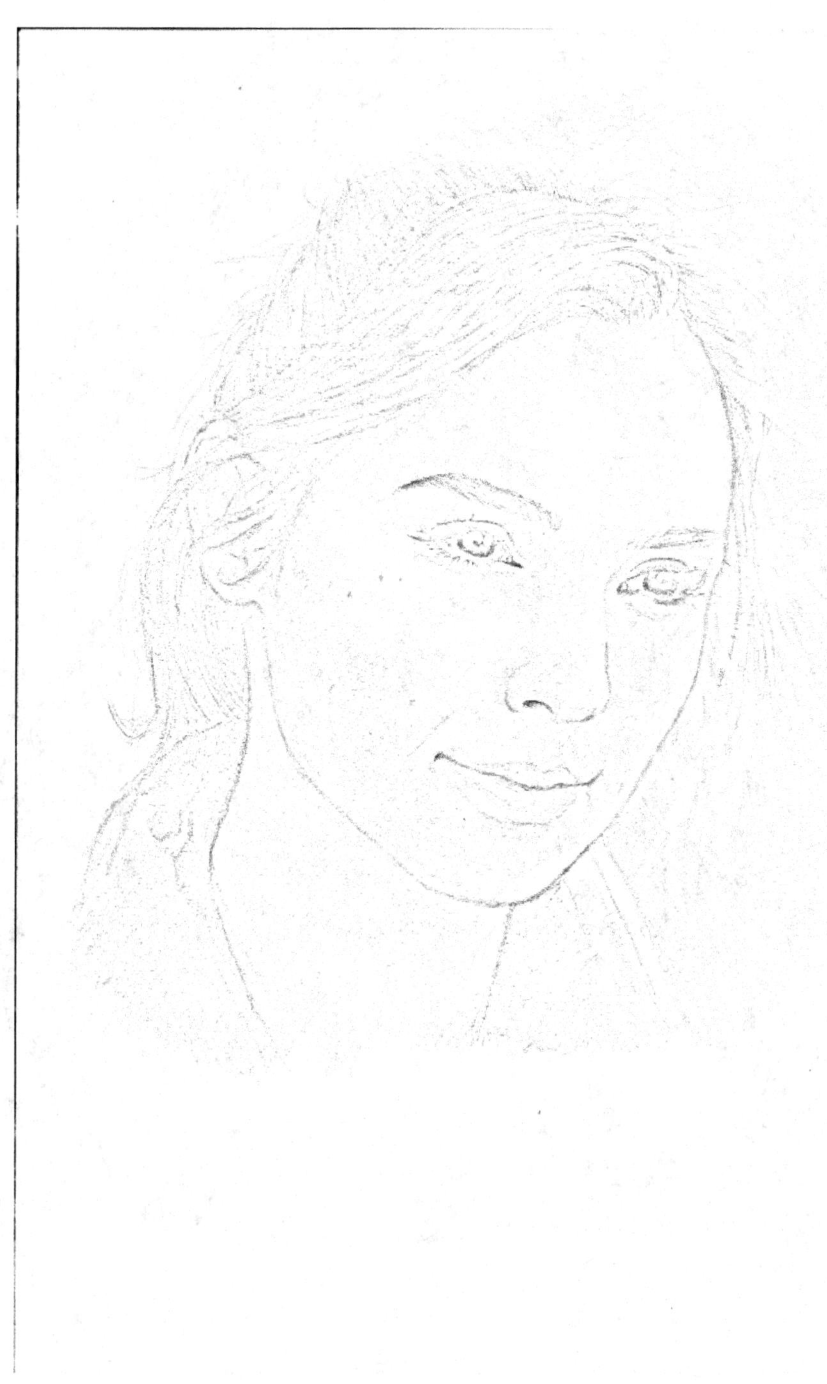

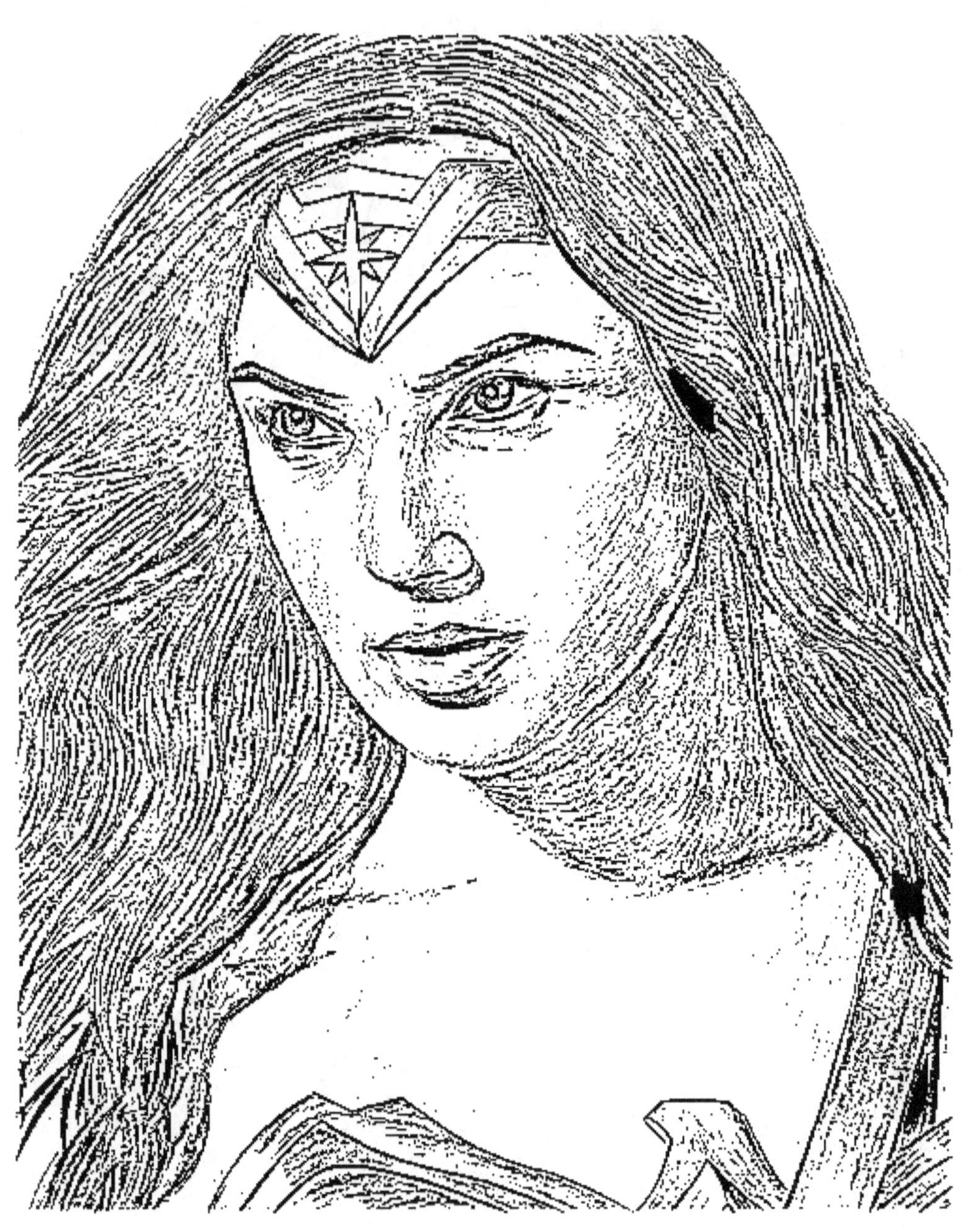

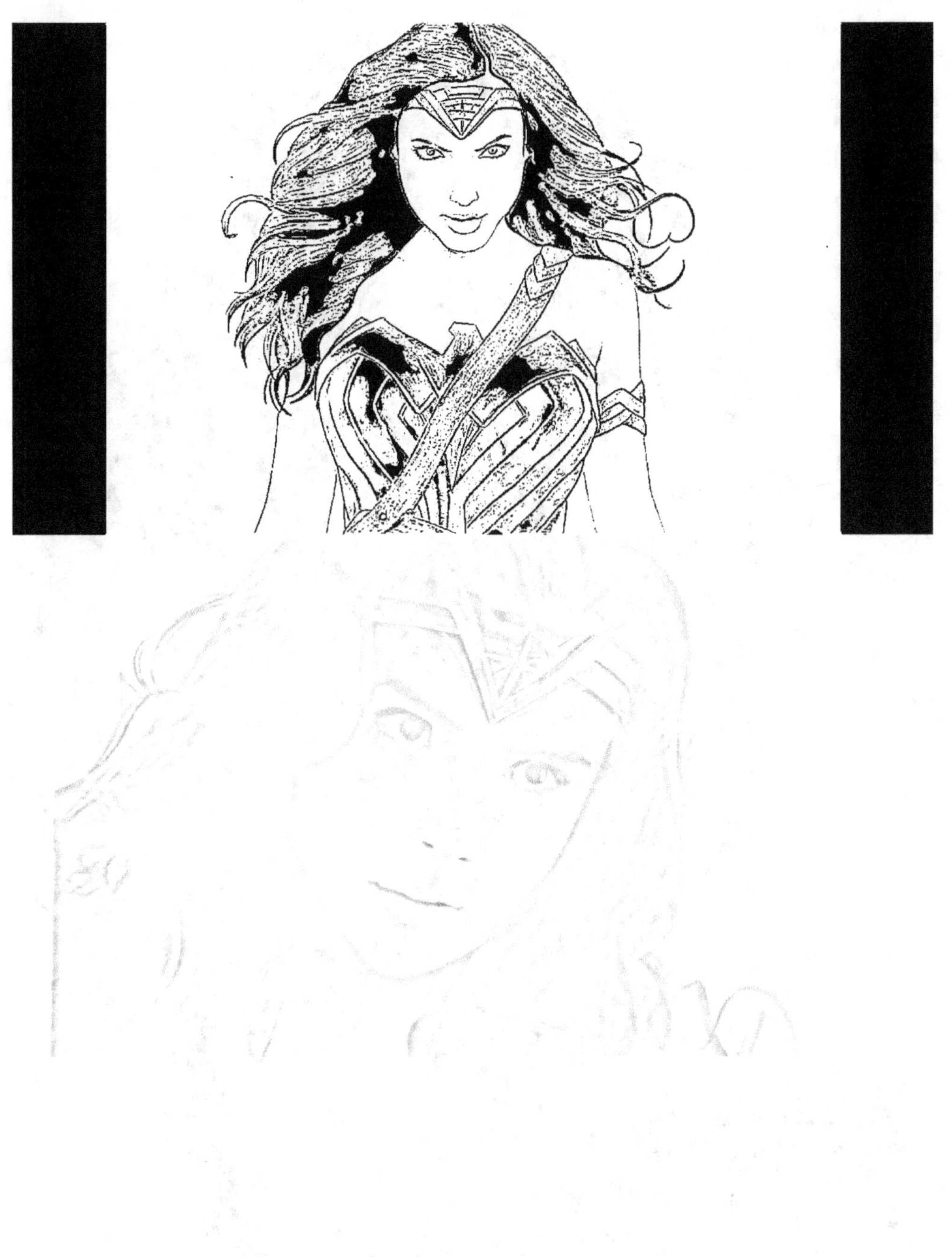

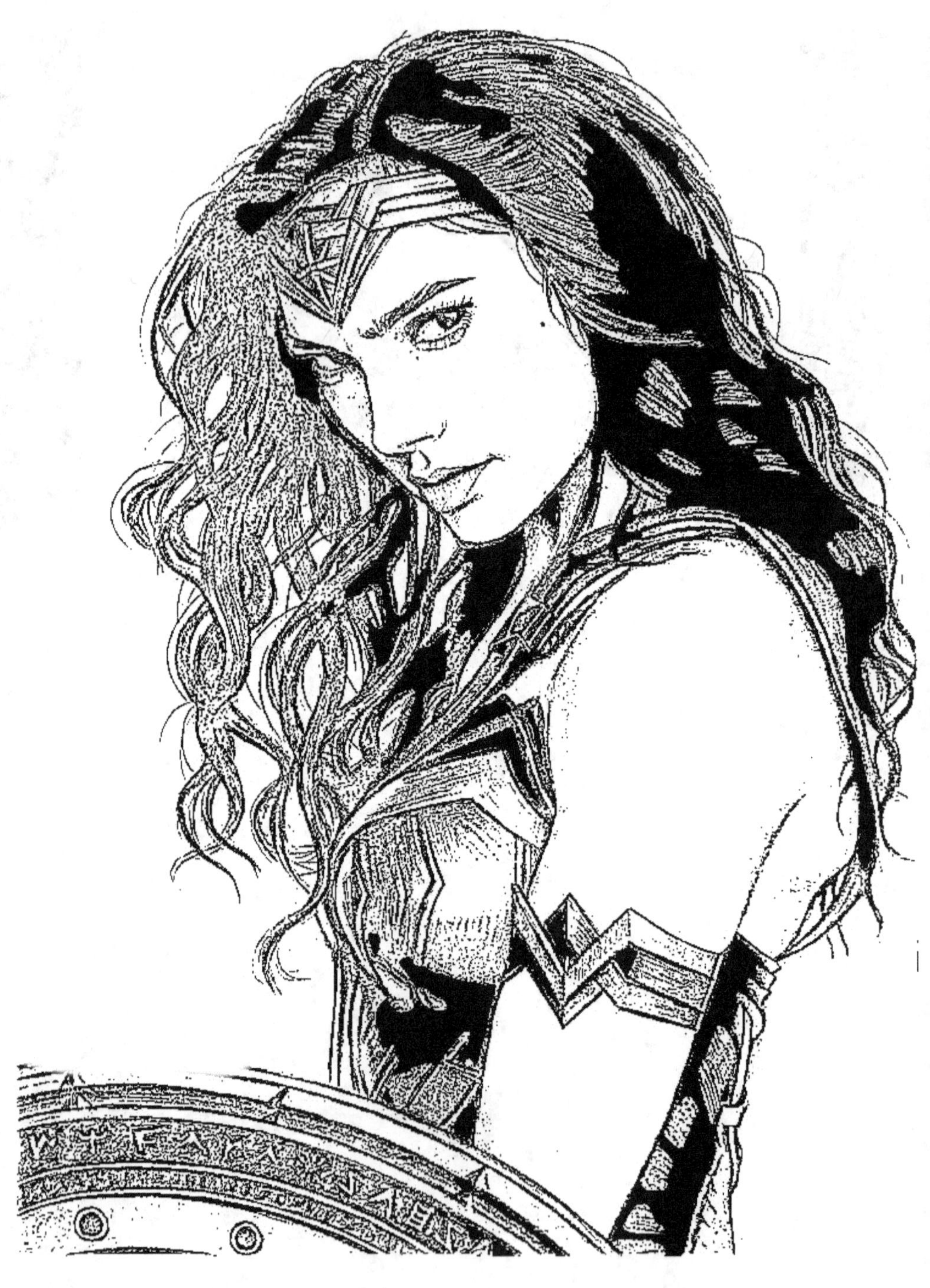

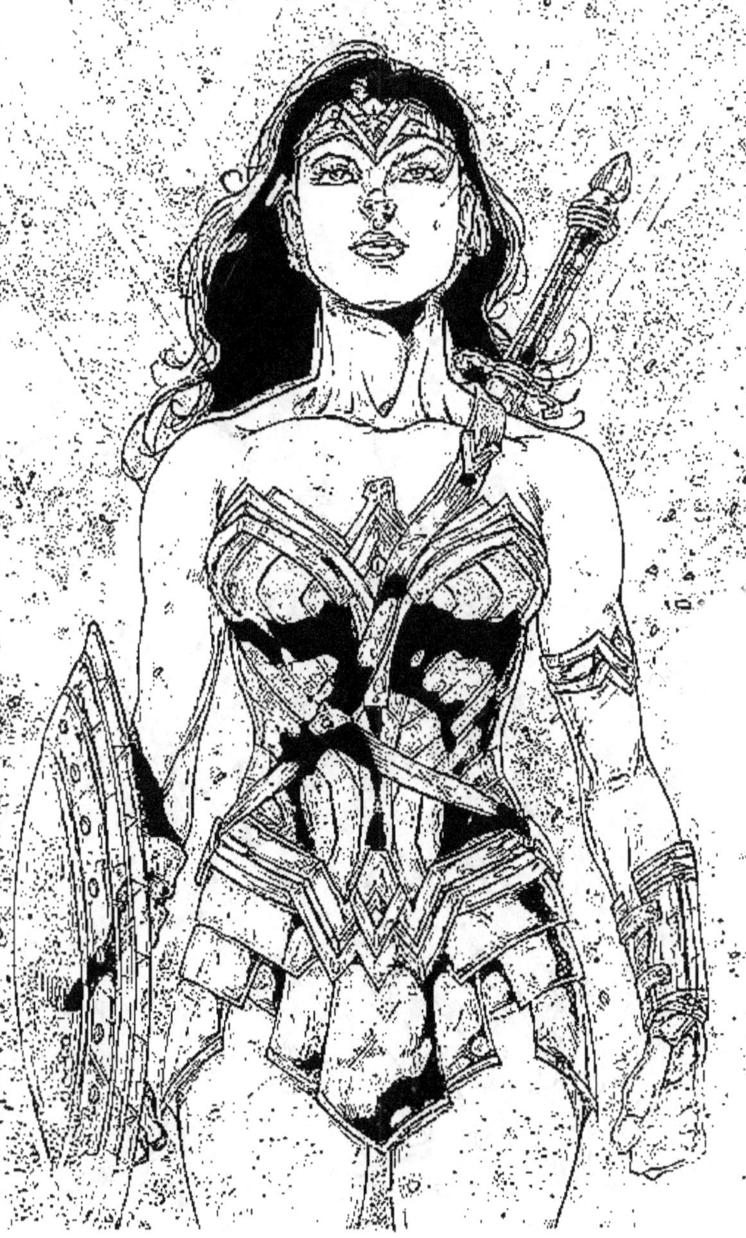

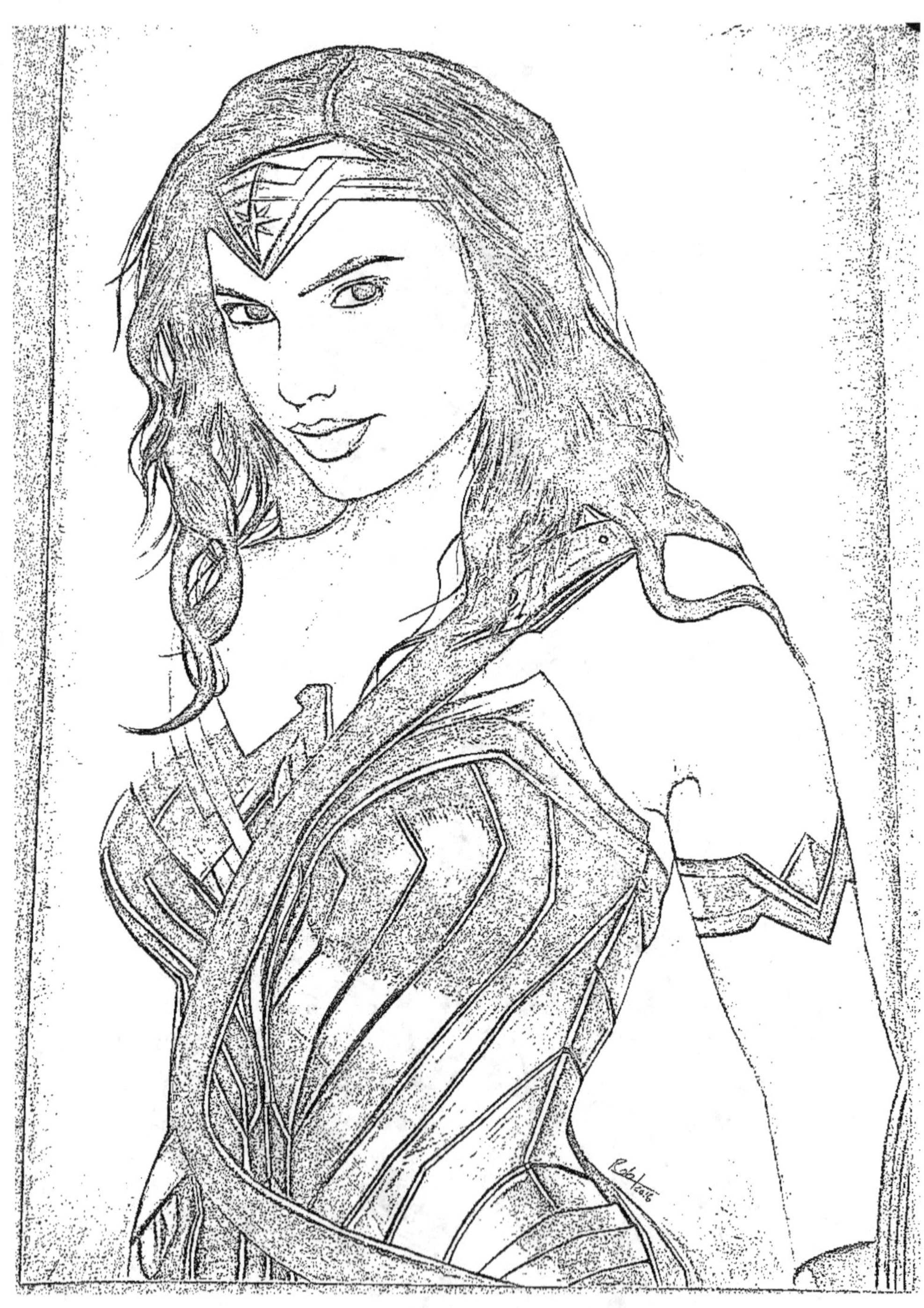

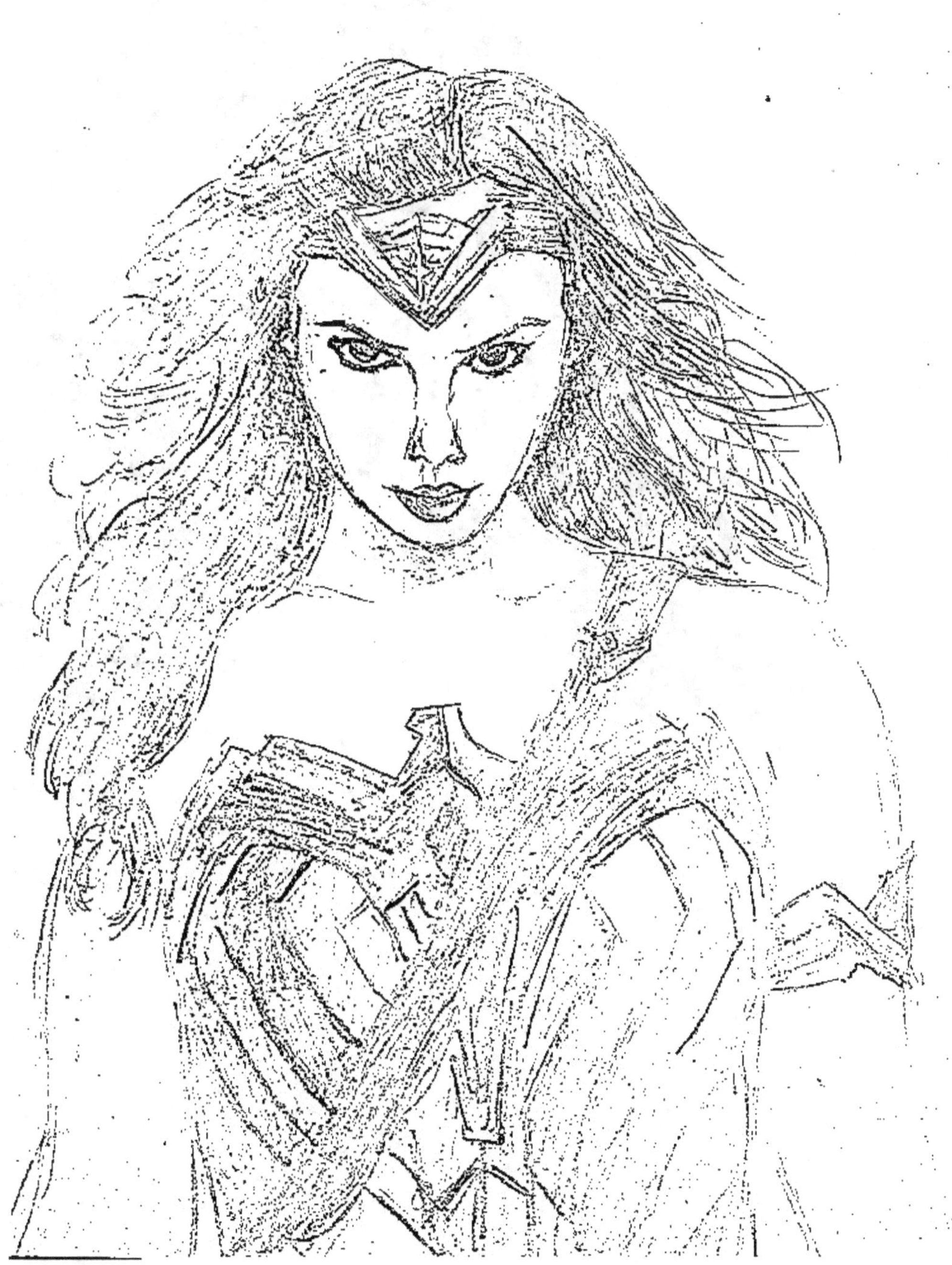

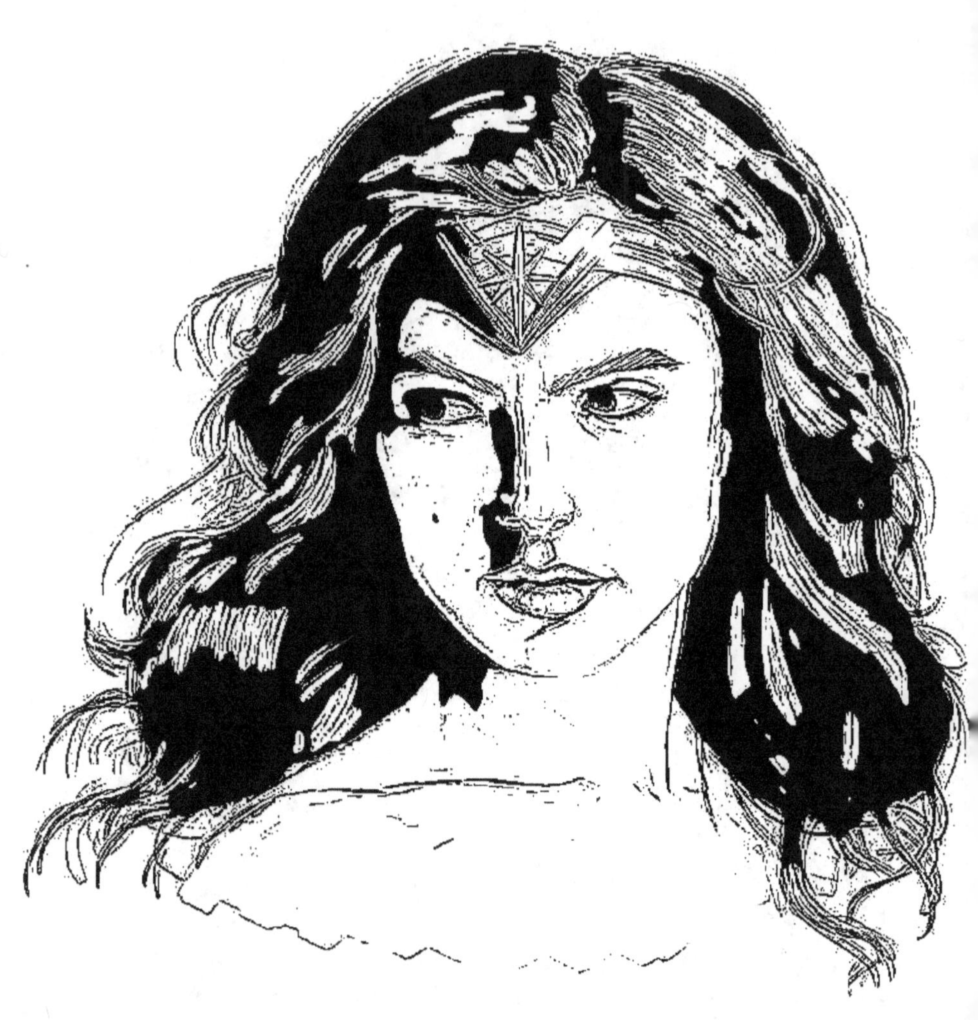

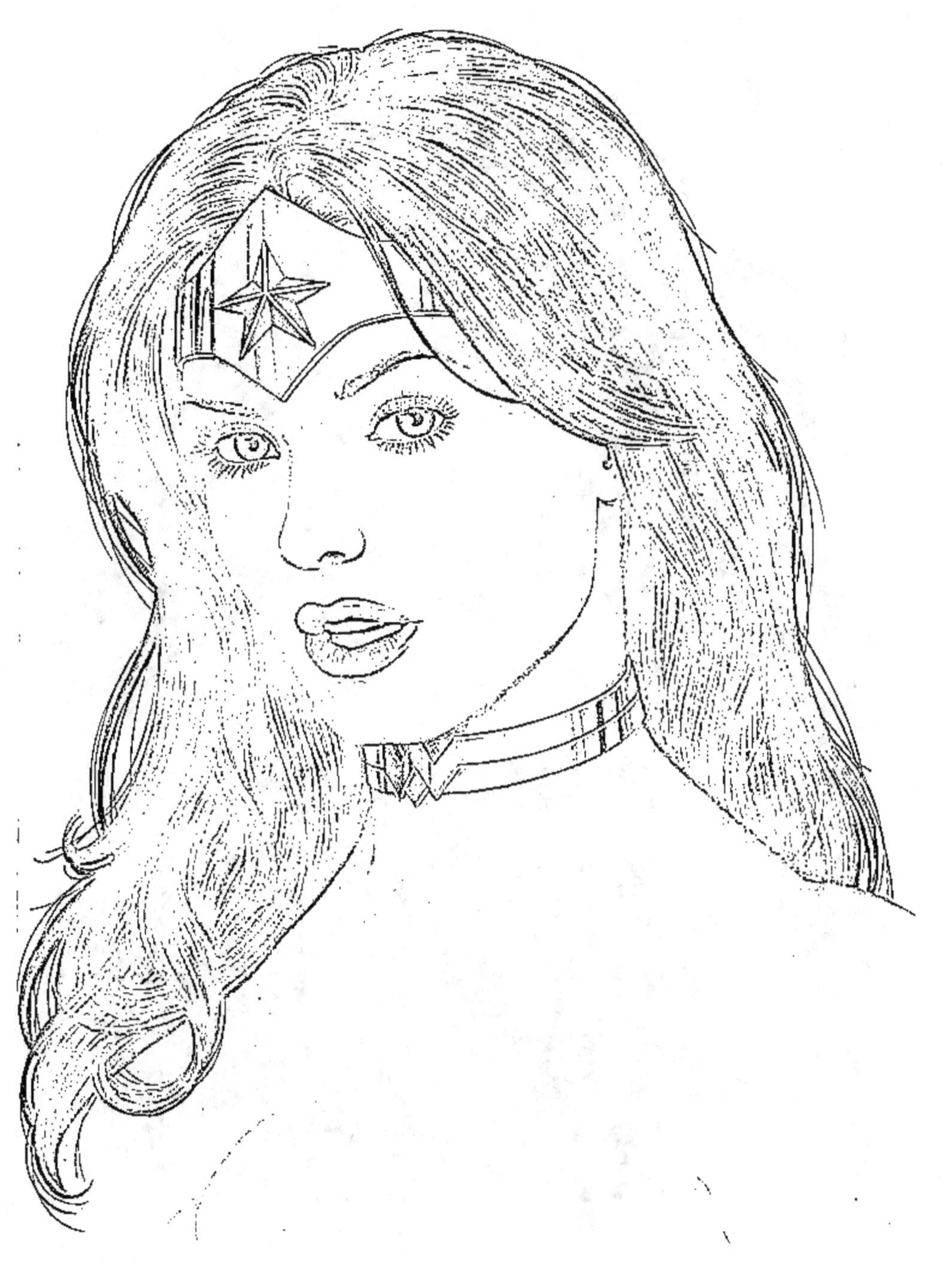

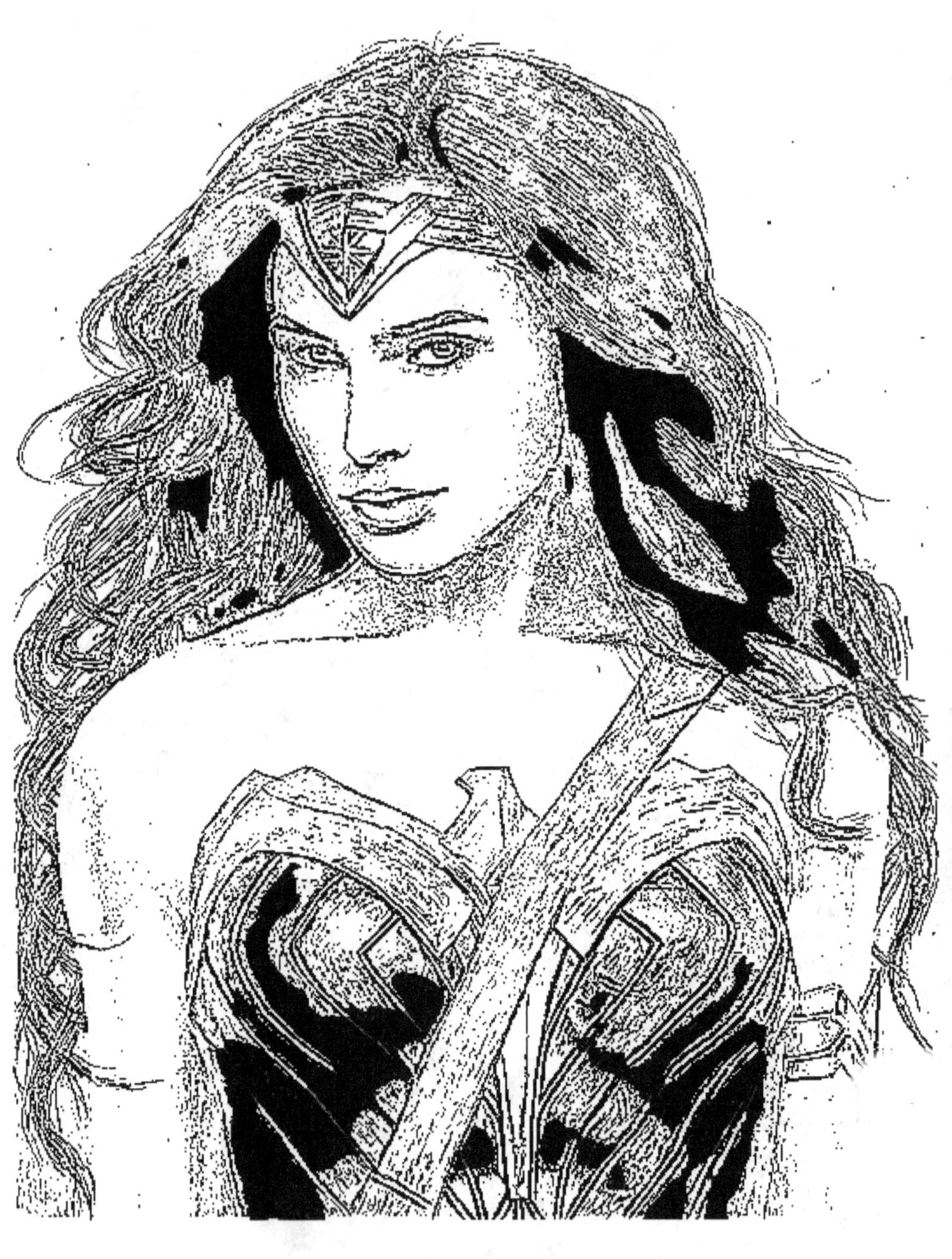

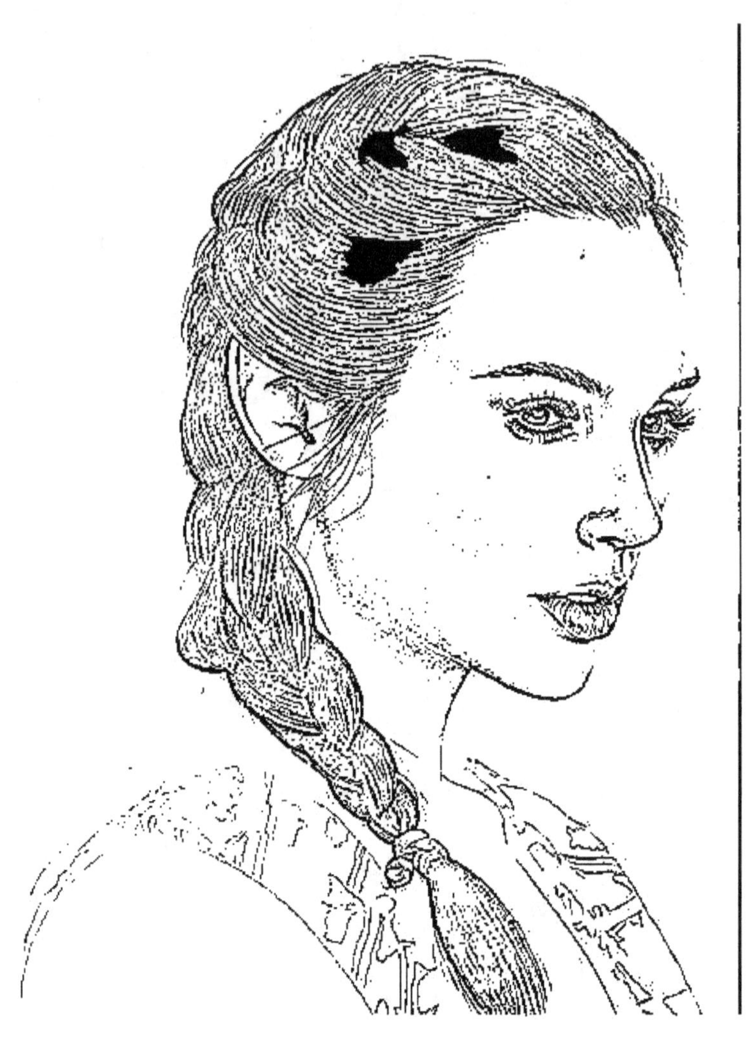

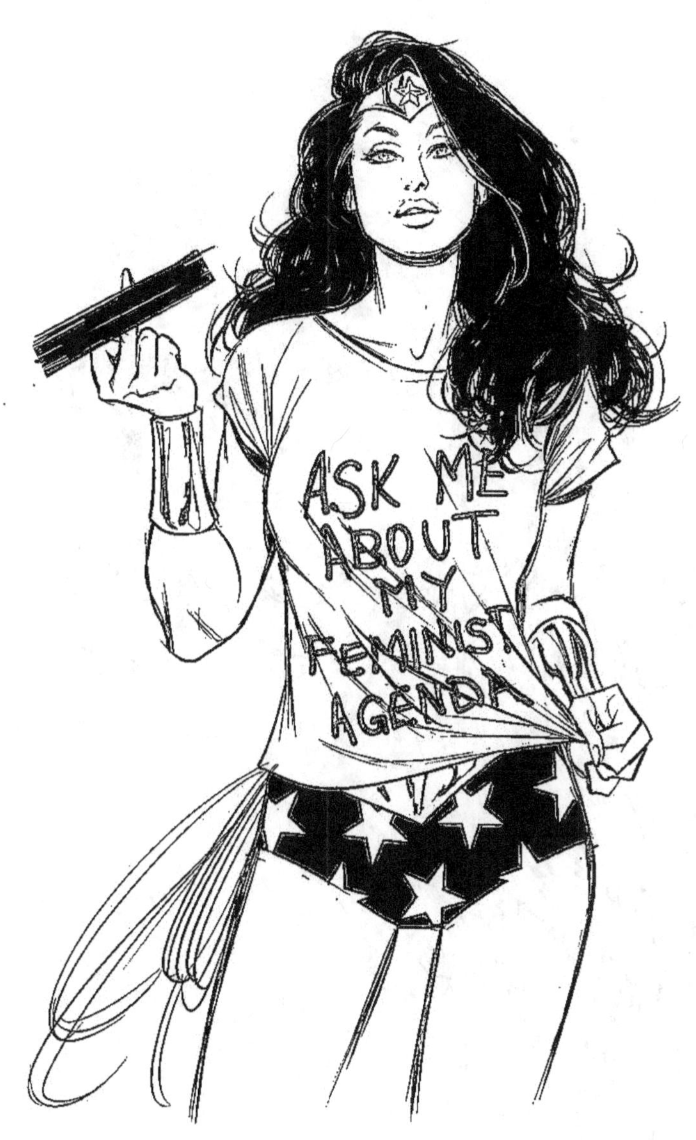

ASK ME
ABOUT
MY
FEMINIST
AGENDA

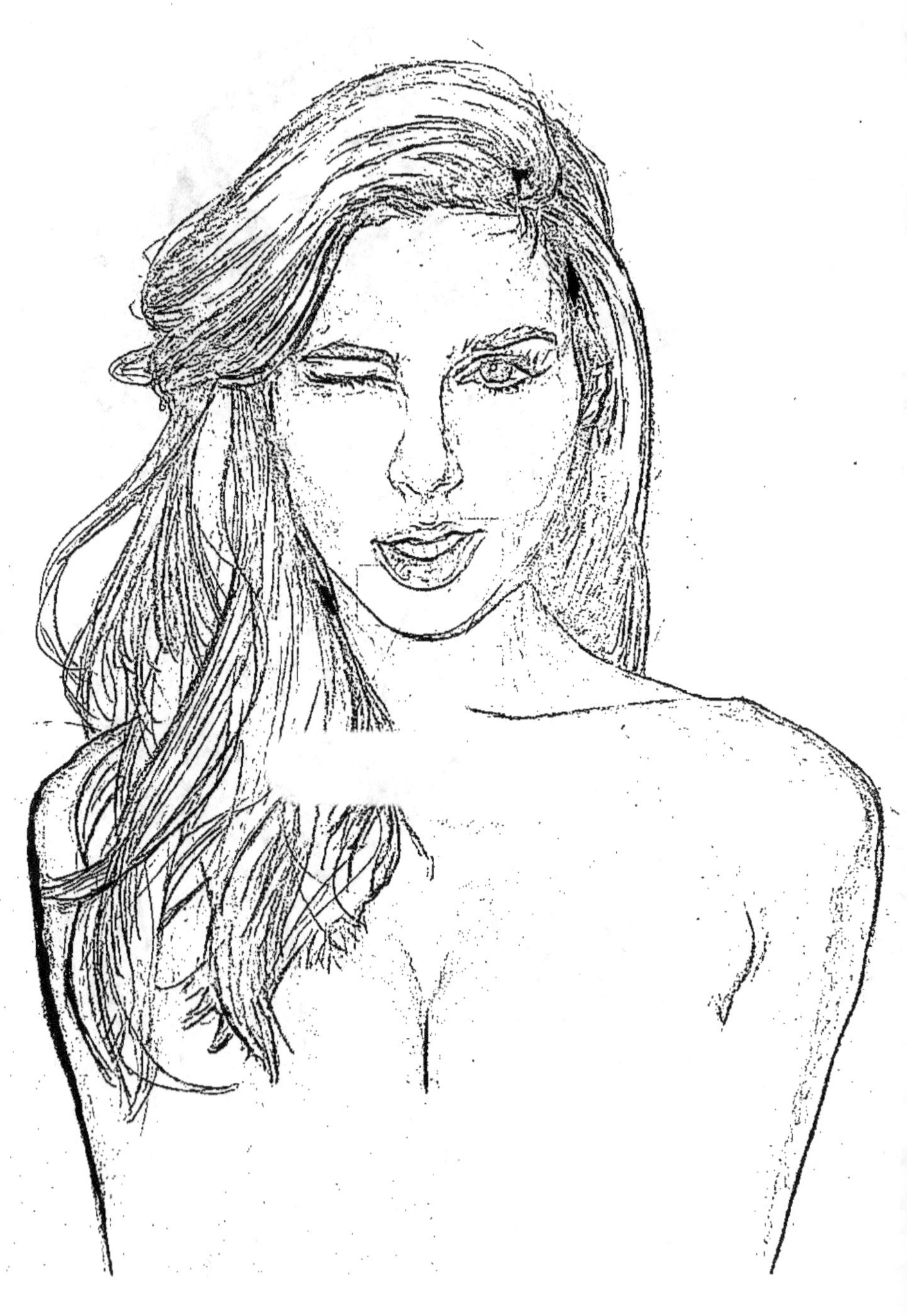

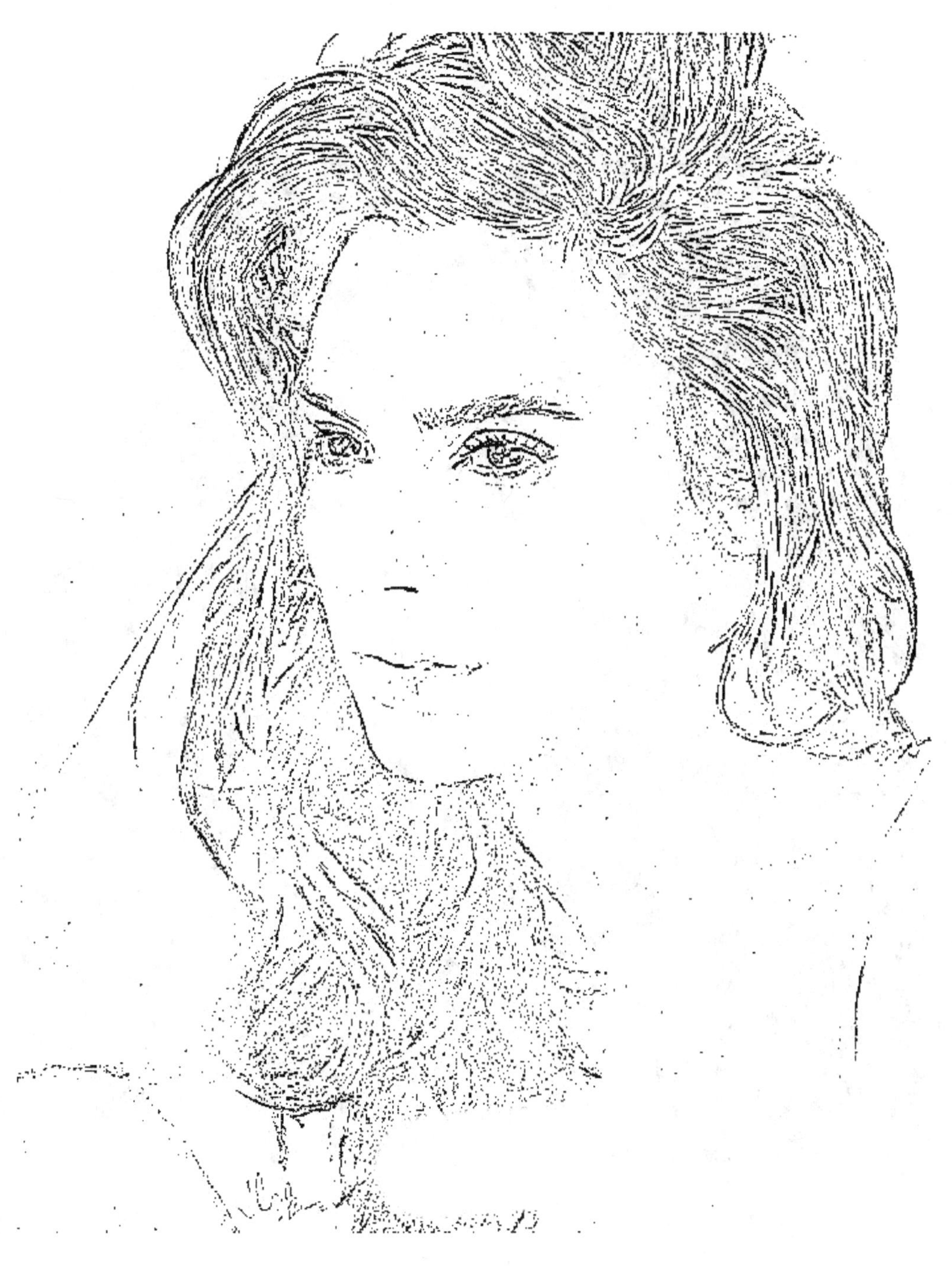

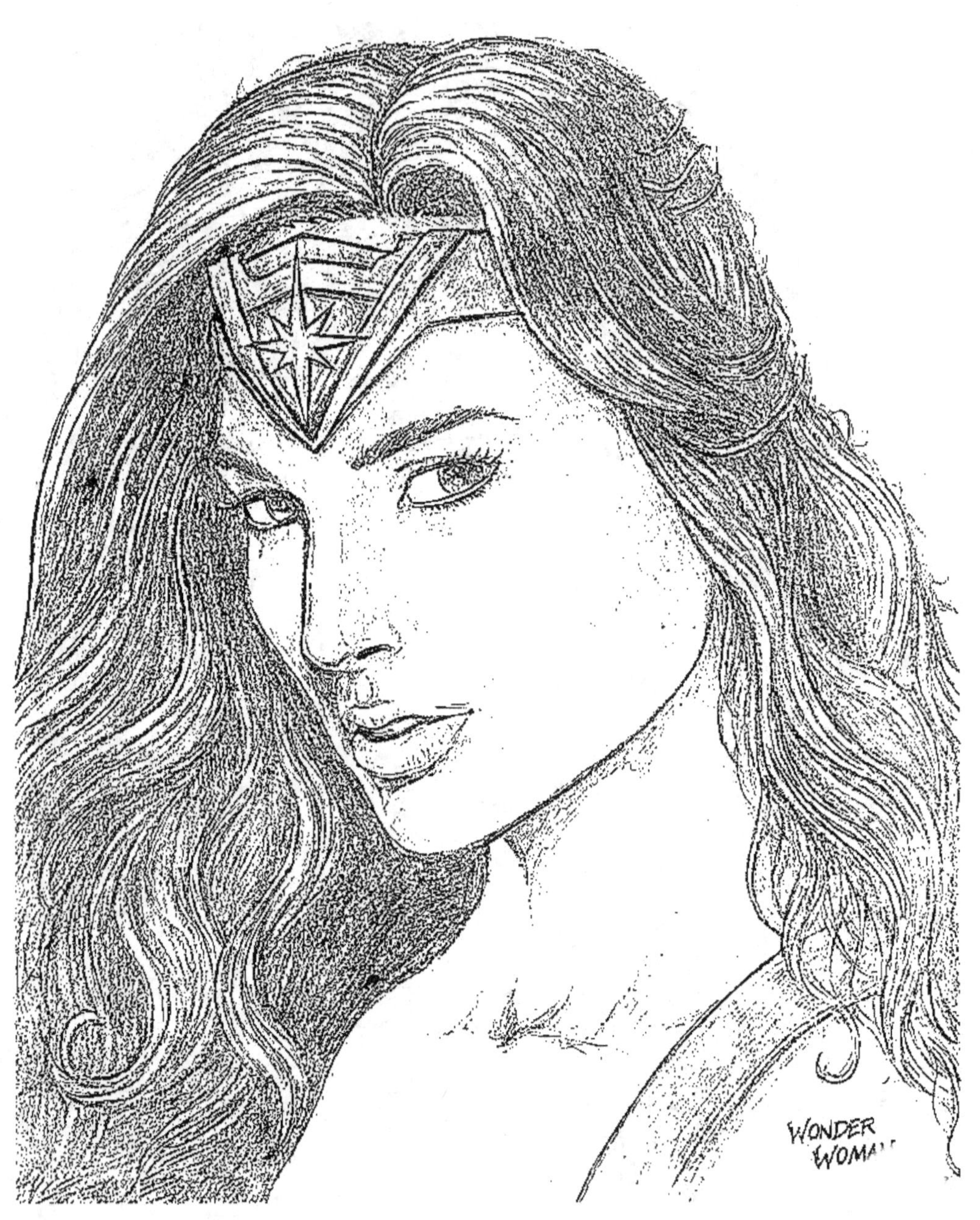

WONDER
WOMAN

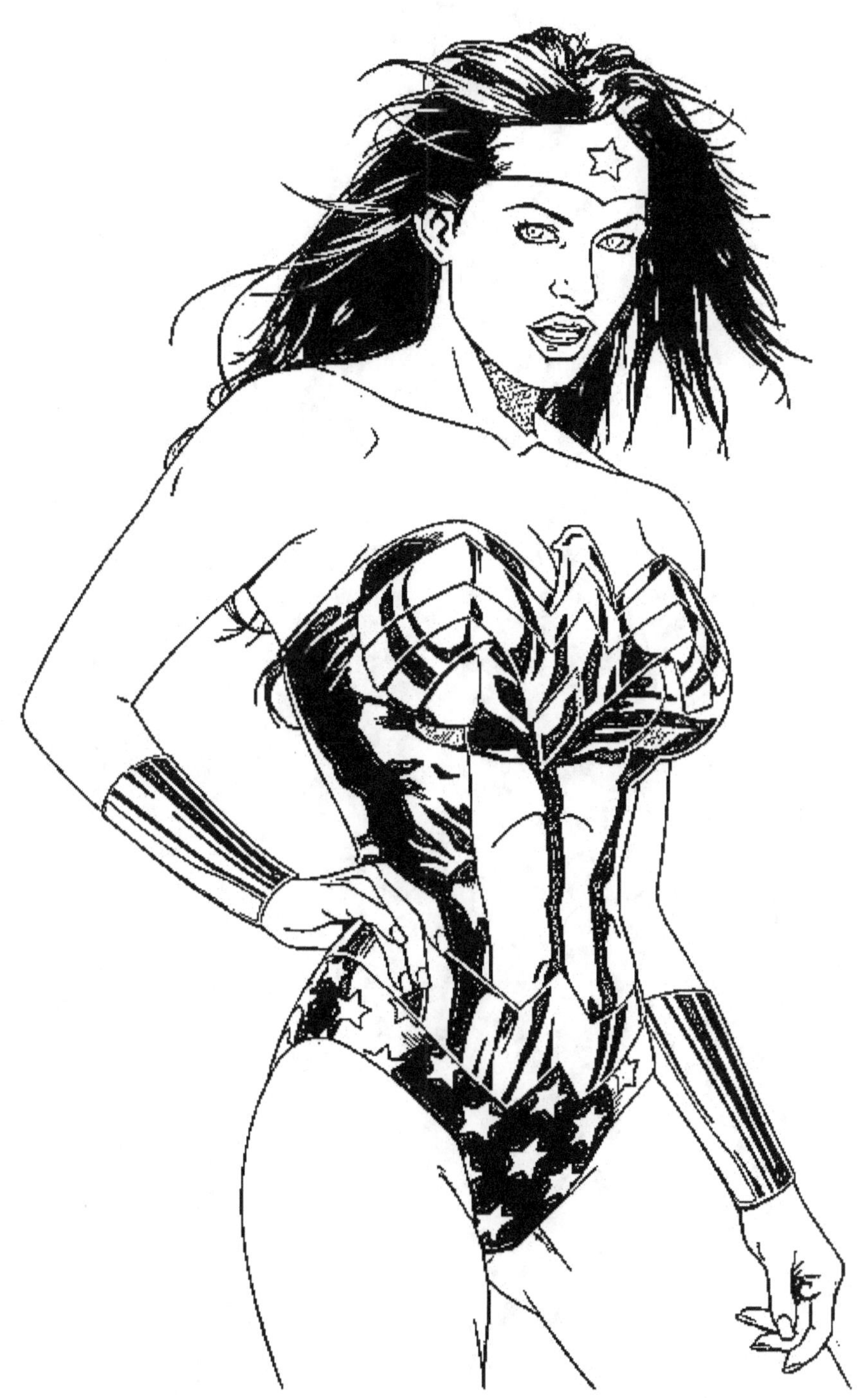